★ OXFORD ★
IN THE CIVIL WAR

★OXFORD★

IN THE CIVIL WAR

Battle for a Vanquished Land

STEPHEN ENZWEILER

Charleston London

THE
History
PRESS

Published by The History Press
Charleston, SC 29403
www.historypress.net

Copyright © 2010 by Stephen Enzweiler
All rights reserved

Front cover: Courtesy of University of Mississippi Special Collections.

Back cover: Courtesy of University of Mississippi Special Collections and the Library of
Congress.

First published 2010

Manufactured in the United States

ISBN 978.1.59629.318.2

Library of Congress CIP data applied for.

To my mother, Virginia Enzweiler, who taught me to love history.

CONTENTS

ACKNOWLEDGEMENTS

I am grateful to many people and organizations for their help in the researching of this book. They served as my north stars, guiding me through the shadowy world of long ago and helping me to bring back to life those prominent citizens of Oxford as they rushed headlong into the fiery travail of secession and war.

In the course of my research, I was introduced to primary source material by outstanding staffs at several libraries. I especially wish to thank the University of Mississippi's Special Collections and Archives at the J.D. Williams Library, most notably Jennifer Ford, Pamela Williamson and archivists Greg Johnson, Jason Kovari, Stephanie McKnight, Leigh McWhite and John Wall, all of whom guided me as I sifted through endless boxes of period papers, letters, diaries, books and other material. I also owe thanks to University of Mississippi's Audrey Uffner, who shared with me her thoughts on sectionalism and secession in antebellum Lafayette County. My gratitude likewise goes to Joe and Becky Murphey, who contributed their unrivaled historical expertise and who introduced me to the Skipwith Historical and Genealogical Society, of which I am now a member. A special thanks to Felicia Pegues and Dr. Will St. Amand of the Skipwith Historical and Genealogical Society for their friendship and help in guiding me through the vast collections of historical material.

Thanks to the Office of the Chancellor of the University of Mississippi and to Shirley Stuart for helping with historical information about the campus buildings of the period. I also want to recognize the many libraries and organizations throughout the country that helped me in my research.

ACKNOWLEDGEMENTS

In Mississippi, the Mississippi Department of Archives and History; Lafayette County Public Library; Skipwith Historical and Genealogical Society; Oxford–Lafayette County Heritage Foundation; Vicki Bishop and Ashley Atkinson at the Oxford City Hall; Oxford Convention and Visitor's Bureau; Corinth Convention and Visitor's Bureau; the Corinth Civil War Interpretive Center; and Mr. Tom Preston of the National Park Service. In Tennessee, Shiloh National Military Park. In Washington, the Library of Congress and the National Archives. In New York, Columbia University Library Manuscript Collections. In Kentucky, Boone County Library and Kenton County Library.

Several friends and colleagues in Oxford and Lafayette County were greatly generous with their time and resources. These include members of the University Greys Camp 1803, Sons of Confederate Veterans, filmmaker and Nathan Bedford Forrest historian Jon Rawl, filmmaker and University Greys expert Micah Ginn and Civil War historian and author Shelby Foote. Thanks also to Richard Murph for his help in researching Jacob Thompson.

There are many who read portions of the manuscript along the way who deserve my gratitude for their comments and suggestions, including Anthony Eichhorn, Jerry Schrepfer, Dave Stadtlander, Aven Whittington and the Honorable Linda Whittington. Thanks also to Keith Sisson, who opened his home and gave me a place to work for as long as necessary while living in Oxford. A special thanks to Woods Eastland of Staple Cotton for providing information on antebellum cotton markets and pricing.

I wish to say a special thanks to my editor Will McKay, my copy editor Amber Allen and the men and women at The History Press for their expertise and for all they did to help this project go from basic concept to manuscript to final book form.

Finally, no amount of thanks is sufficient to express gratitude to my sweet wife, Patty Enzweiler, who diligently read and edited each page from first to final draft and who unflinchingly encouraged me every step of the way.

Oxford, Mississippi
July 2010

INTRODUCTION

In the Course of Human Events

"Prudence, indeed, will dictate that governments long established should not be changed for light and transient causes."
—*Declaration of Independence, July 4, 1776*

In 1834, a twenty-four-year-old, newly minted lawyer named Jacob Thompson rode into Pontotoc, Mississippi, for the first time. The son of a wealthy North Carolina planter, he came, like so many other white settlers from the east, to buy land, grow cotton and get rich. He was only one of thousands who made the journey in what became one of the greatest human migrations in American frontier history. The land that once belonged to the Chickasaw Indians was quickly flooded with white settlers like Thompson, full of energy, high expectations and solemn purpose. They spread out over the rich fertile landscape south of the Tallahatchie, laying claim to vast reaches of territory. Within only a few short years, they managed to completely transform the rugged high prairie landscape of scrub oak, cedar and pine forest into one of the most valuable and productive agricultural regions in the nation. On it they cultivated the cotton that became the white gold of the 1850s, making the planters who grew it extremely wealthy and turning the United States into a leading economic power. All it took was land and slaves.

The seminal event that set it all in motion occurred on May 26, 1830, when President Andrew Jackson signed into law the Indian Removal Act, opening the door for white settlement in the west. For northern Mississippi, the first fruits born of the act came in 1832 in the form of the Treaty of

Pontotoc Creek, in which the Chickasaw nation ceded to the United States government more than 6,422,400 acres in Indian land—a sprawling territory consisting of roughly the northernmost quarter of the state. The pioneers who settled Lafayette County in the 1830s would ultimately carry forward the ideals of Jacksonian democracy, and the land of the Chickasaws would ultimately fade into the ether of history as the forests south of the Tallahatchie were cleared, built upon and cultivated until it was no longer recognizable as having ever belonged to the Chickasaws. What remained was the on-rushing preoccupation of a people consumed with the politics of cotton and slaves, defining forever the lives of its residents in the years that led up to secession and war.

It was a period of unprecedented economic growth and prosperity for the people of Lafayette County. In 1859—the last year reliable records were kept before war began—there were 1,043 landowners in Lafayette County cultivating 335,585 acres, which produced a record 19,282 bales of cotton at a value of $1,195,484. American cotton by then accounted for more than half of all American exports, supplying 75 percent of Britain's textile industry and nearly three-fourths of the world's total cotton demand.

But it all came at a price. By the time the Southern states seceded, slavery had been a way of life in America for over 250 years. Although its morality was increasingly in question, few of the citizens in Oxford in 1860 could ever have imagined a world without it. For them, the existence of slavery was ordained by God and nature, a normal feature of American society, engraved in their minds and carved into their souls as deep and irremovable as if chiseled into granite. As an institution, it was regulated under strict legality and constitutionality—an economic and political practice so interwoven into everyday American life that the two could not be separated from each other without catastrophic results. Slavery, then, became like the single cotter pin that held together the grand assemblage of national agricultural machinery, which, if the pin was pulled from the security of its keeper, would cause the whole assemblage to fly apart in its own destruction.

In trying to tell the story of Oxford during the Civil War, I discovered, not surprisingly, that slavery was that cotter pin, the single most omnipresent feature of life in Lafayette County. In the letters and diaries of the people who lived here, they wrote copiously of their need for slaves to take care of even the most minute duties. One cannot help but recognize in it the deep irony that the white population itself was, in many ways, enslaved to the institution of slavery. Taking it a step further, the war that came in 1861 became a war to free the South from its own enslavement to a system from which it was otherwise not able to free itself. Twenty-five years after Oxford's founding, the pioneers who built Lafayette County into an agricultural dynamo would find themselves standing at the doorstep of a great war, led by political extremists and fire-eating secessionists caught up in the revolutionary struggle for Southern independence. In the decade of the 1850s, slavery had gone from a perpetual institution ordained by God and protected by the Constitution to one seen as a great evil and a tragic scar upon the face of society.

In my own attempt to comprehend the meaning and significance of the Civil War as it occurred in Oxford, I did not wish to present the story as merely a description of battles, strategies and troop movements. People are what make the history, and my desire was to tell the story of the war through the lives of the local people who lived it. Among those who appear in these pages are three distinct generations of Oxford residents. The most senior of those are the pioneer citizens, among them Jacob and Kate Thompson, Alexander and Rebecca Pegues, Judge James M. Howry, William Turner, Dr. Thomas Dudley Isom, Burlina W. Butler and William S. Neilsen. They were the early settlers who quite literally built Oxford and Lafayette County from the ground up. Then came Lucius Quintus Cincinnatus Lamar, Frederick A. Barnard, Augustus B. Longstreet and Dr. Henry Branham, who arrived during the boom times in the 1840s and 1850s after the University of Mississippi was established, when times were good and cotton was king. The youngest generation consisted of the university students—Jeremiah Gage, Jim Dailey, James F. Dooley, Thomas P. Buford and William B. Lowry— typical college kids who attended classes, courted pretty girls and struggled over exams, and who, when the time came, would all band together and rush off to war in search of glory. The slaves of Lafayette County are distinctly their own story, apart and separate from the rest. Yet it would not be truthful for me to omit their contribution in these pages, since their experience is at the center of the story of Oxford and the Civil War. Among the former slaves whose stories I am privileged to tell are those of Joanna Thompson Isom, Polly Turner Cancer, Lucindy Hall Shaw, "Aunt" Jane Wilburn and a murdered slave named John.

It soon became clear, however, that two particular individuals emerged as representatives of two kinds of destinies the Civil War seemed to produce. By all measure, Jacob Thompson was a skilled national politician fluent in the art of political survival at the time the war began. But by 1862, he unexplainably became a target of Secretary of War Edwin M. Stanton. Stanton, like many Northerners at the time, was convinced that secession had been a Southern conspiracy, created by its leadership and propagated by fire-eating politicians and extremists. As a former secretary of the interior before secession, Jacob Thompson fell under immediate suspicion. Stanton's efforts to vilify Thompson, along with Jefferson Davis, Clement C. Clay and other Southern leaders, generated greater public support for the war at a time when things were going badly for the Union. In practice and in effect, Stanton became the first great spin doctor of the media, feeding Northern newspapers with carefully written stories aimed at deliberate character assassination, with the eventual aim—if the North won—of prosecuting the guilty for treason.

Thompson's own plight began during the Union army's invasion of northern Mississippi with the deliberate theft by General Ulysses S. Grant of his personal papers, which Grant sent directly to Stanton in Washington. This deliberate act seemed to be the tipping point for Thompson, who afterward began engaging in more unpredictable and clandestine behavior. Although he traveled extensively throughout 1862 and 1863, little is known of his whereabouts or activities until 1864, when he accepted Jefferson Davis's offer to head Confederate spy operations in Canada. It was a decision that seemed out of character for a man like Thompson, yet it was one that would haunt him for the rest of his life. His distinguished prewar record in national politics contrasts substantially with his later wartime life as a spymaster. In addition to his profound failure in that role, Thompson ultimately was implicated and charged as a co-conspirator in the assassination of Abraham Lincoln. Though the allegations eventually were proven false, it still leaves us with a picture of two Jacob Thompsons—one as the deft, calculating politician, a powerful and influential figure on the national stage; and another, darker Jacob Thompson, one who was not above desperate acts of conspiracy, secrecy and perhaps even murder. And so, for us he remains an enigma, an Oxford founding father, who abandoned the town he helped build and the friends he once knew. Perhaps he no longer cared; he was nearing sixty and still a very wealthy man. In the end, he withdrew from society and divorced himself from politics entirely, either unable or unwilling to accept the war's outcome or to effect any measure of reconciliation.

Lucius Quintus Cincinnatus Lamar by contrast, rose like a phoenix from the ashes of destruction, completely changed by the experience of war. The former fire-eater reentered national politics in the early 1870s and was elected to his old seat in the House of Representatives, then elected to the Senate and subsequently appointed secretary of the interior. Finally, at fifty-three, he was appointed a justice to the Supreme Court of the United

States. From the events of the war, he had learned a great truth—that to serve the South one must above all else be devoted to the nation to which the South belongs. While many of his fellow Southerners criticized him for his attempts to repair the national rupture the Civil War had wrought, he found redemption on both a personal and national level in the work of postwar reconciliation, a master credo and political ideology he professed as the only solution to the South's postwar plight. Long after the turn of the twentieth century, Lamar's legacy continued to command a large following and has become the model for the type of public service, national policy and individual behavior exemplified by his efforts at reconciliation not just between North and South, but between whole races and cultures of man.

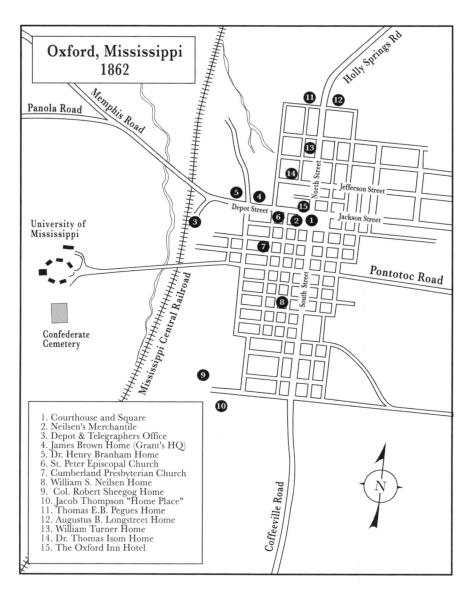

Map of Oxford, Mississippi 1862. *Courtesy of the author.*

CHAPTER 1

THE STARS IN
THEIR COURSES

"A people with such a spirit cannot be subdued."
—*Jacob Thompson, June 7, 1861*

By June of 1857, there still seemed to be hope of salvaging the situation. At least Jacob Thompson believed there was, as did most of the Democratic Party leaders who were assembled around the dinner table at his home in Oxford. They came as a result of a crisis that had been brewing in northern Mississippi's First Congressional District—that of Democratic incumbent Daniel B. Wright's decision not to run for reelection to Congress. It was a potentially ruinous turn of events, one that created some panic throughout the district and in Jackson. The political leadership insisted that only a Democratic Party presence in Congress could secure a proper defense of their Southern rights. But the delegation at Holly Springs had so far failed to produce a suitable nominee. Wright's unexpected decision left the party's political jugular exposed as opposition party candidates seized the initiative and began waging an effective campaign against them. Of most concern were the aggressive efforts by conservative Whigs and by one particular antisecessionist opponent from the American Know-Nothing party named James Lusk Alcorn.

At the same time, Thompson was still licking his own wounds after a stinging defeat in his second bid to win a seat in the U.S. Senate, losing this time to his fellow Mississippian Jefferson Davis. It had been his latest attempt to revive a stalled career in national politics, having previously served as a congressman in the House of Representatives for six successive terms from 1839 until 1851. Now he assembled all the party bosses and political insiders at his home to discuss what could be done for the First District. Few in Democratic-rich northern Mississippi needed to argue the importance of holding onto this particular congressional seat. Representation in Congress by Southern Democrats had always been the surest guarantee of protecting the rights and agricultural interests of the South, especially after 1850 as King Cotton rose to dominate the U.S. and global economies. As far back as any of them could remember, Democrats had held the majority in both houses of Congress. For years, Southerners believed such an arrangement must be kept, for it defended slavery and protected the agricultural system under which they lived. It was this system of cultivating and producing cotton that had risen to become the source and summit of the South's entire economic and political power.

But in Jacob Thompson's view, the defection of the Democratic incumbent was just one more symptom of the weakening hold Southern Democrats held on sectional politics. Most Southerners blamed it on the Republican Party, a fledgling amalgamation of former Whigs, antislavery Democrats, Northern radicals and conservatives formed in the early 1850s. Their common purpose was to prevent the spread of slavery into new territories and to enforce the abolition of slavery where it already existed. This pro-Negro stance earned them the nickname Black Republicans. By the time of the passage of the Kansas–Nebraska Act in 1854, public sentiment about the issue had reached a full boil, resulting in Bleeding Kansas. Sectional violence erupted in the new territory and became the new rallying cry for the Northern antislavery movement. The killing that resulted in Kansas caused an irreparable rupture in the national political dialogue on the question of slavery in the new territories, and it would continue to be a central focus of sectionalist debate throughout the nation as the country polarized toward war.

Assembled at Jacob Thompson's table were some of the local Democratic Party's political power hitters—men like Roger Barton, Benjamin F. Dill, James Brown, W.F. Avent and the powerful and influential Judge James Howry. Wealthy planter and Mississippi state senator Alexander Pegues was there, as was the respected Oxford physician Dr. Thomas Dudley Isom. All of them were wealthy men, planters, slaveholders and politically connected. But Thompson had his eye on only one man. At the end of the table casually sipping wine was a thirty-one-year-old lawyer and former Georgia state legislator named Lucius Quintus Cincinnatus Lamar.

Although a fairly recent arrival in Oxford, everybody knew Lucius Lamar. Called Lusche by his friends, he was relatively young and politically inexperienced. But none of that mattered when the Georgia-born lawyer opened his mouth to speak before a crowd, his fiery secessionist oratory suddenly spilling out in vibrant, well-aimed argument, earning him the reputation as a fire-eater. The son of a Georgia planter, Lamar came to Oxford in 1849 at the invitation of his father-in-law, Augustus B. Longstreet, the newly appointed president of the University of Mississippi, whose daughter Virginia he had married but two years before. When not on the stump, Lamar was an unassuming figure. He had "a rather tall and full figure," noted the December 26, 1859 edition of the *New York Times*, "…with a large, high forehead bulging out over his face, long, sleek and plentiful brown hair, combed back behind his ears, a reddish-brown beard, shaved on the upper lip, blue eyes with a red tinge in them." As a public

Jacob Thompson, circa 1848. A political moderate, he was one of the most influential politicians in Mississippi. Like his father-in-law, Peyton Jones, few things went on in Lafayette County that Jacob Thompson didn't have some control over. *Courtesy of the Library of Congress.*

speaker, the *Times* went on to describe him as "extremely fiery, and inclined to raise his voice; but his…descriptions are graphic and poetical, extensively colored with Southern war paint, and heightened to an interesting point by many romantic exaggerations."

He was admired by everyone, even by his political opponents. He was always full of new ideas, big dreams and sudden impulses, and he possessed "a capacity for the most enduring and strongest friendships." According to Mrs. Clement C. Clay, he often expressed his endearment to friends in quaint ways. "I have seen him walk softly up behind Mr. Clay, touch him lightly on the shoulder, and as my husband turned quickly to see what was wanted, 'Lusche'…would kiss him suddenly and lightly on the forehead."

Lucius Quintus Cincinnatus Lamar, 1861. This portrait was taken shortly after Mississippi seceded from the Union. "I war upon your government!" he shouted from the floor of the House only the year before. "I am against it! I raise then the banner of secession, and I will fight under it as long as the blood flows and ebbs in my veins." *Courtesy of Special Collections, University of Mississippi Libraries.*

His sensitive nature, however, had its drawbacks. Like his father, he suffered from deep bouts of depression, a trait that prompted his friends to nickname him Moody Lamar. Yet, beneath the thin, somber veneer lay a powder keg of passionate, inspired oratory described by some as part devil and part genius, and when he rose to speak, his eyes became like two glowing coals, his mouth cavernous and unassailable, speaking with sweeping gestures and in daring language that was "impetuous, scholarly, defiant."

But while Lamar's oratorical prowess made him a rising star on the political horizon, it also had its drawbacks. Many in the legislature dreaded his secessionist ranting on the chamber floor, and it was known on more than one occasion that he had to be practically muzzled by his fellow Democrats during some of his vehement anti-Northern tirades. His political views at the time were often considered "narrow and sectionalist" by his critics. But in his defense, he claimed he was only defending his principles that were the birthright of every Southerner. "Others may boast of their widely extended patriotism and their enlarged and comprehensive love of this union," he later explained in one of his first speeches in Congress. "With me I confess that the promotion of Southern interests is second in importance only to the preservation of Southern honor."

At Jacob Thompson's home, the debate went on well into the evening. More wine was served. The men broke into smaller groups but the discussion failed to reach any firm conclusions. The Democratic nominating convention that had recently met at Holly Springs to select a nominee had become hopelessly deadlocked. When Lamar's name was initially proposed, the convention rejected him as too extremist for the voters. The political environment, asserted the delegates, needed a candidate with more moderate views if Democrats were to have a chance of winning the seat by popular vote. Their concern, they argued, was not to alienate any more possible Democrats who may be riding the fence with extremist talk of secession, which surely it was in Lamar's unpredictable nature to do.

At last, Jacob Thompson rose from the table to speak. "Our choice of a candidate," he confidently began, "must be endowed by genius and culture, with the qualities that make a politician and a statesman. He must be gifted with eloquence and scholarly attainments, and must have no moral or political sins to answer for." The men nodded to one another and rapped their hands on the table in agreement. "He must be ready to meet any question that may arise in an exciting campaign such as this," Thompson continued, "and be able to win the masses over..." Judge Howry stood and addressed the gathering. "Where do we find such a man?" Thompson raised his glass in toast. "Gentlemen," he said, smiling broadly. "I present to you our next Congressman—Lucius Quintus Cincinnatus Lamar!"

At first there was silence. Lamar looked up from his wine. Then, as Thompson's words settled into their minds, it became evident to everyone that Lamar had been the only logical choice all along. He, above all the rest, was best suited for the job if their democratic representation in Congress was to be preserved and if slavery and the rights of Mississippi and of the Southern states were to have any chance of being defended. When the convention next met, Lamar's name was submitted; after the sixtieth ballot, he was nominated by acclamation and went on to win the election by a landslide. Perhaps only Jacob Thompson saw the great irony in the achievement he had just helped to engineer. While he had failed to win his own election to the Senate that fall, Lucius Lamar now occupied the same congressional seat that had once been his.

As the Georgia-born fire-eater set off for the turbulent world of Washington politics, Thompson returned to his quiet life in Oxford, perhaps wondering, as the cold of winter settled once more upon the countryside, just what turn his own life would take. He was getting to be an old man, nearing fifty. Perhaps, he must have mused, his political career was, indeed, over. But not long after, he received word that President-elect James Buchanan, as a reward for Thompson's help in securing his nomination and for campaigning during his successful 1856 presidential campaign, had appointed him to his cabinet as secretary of the interior. Jacob Thompson found himself back in the game. Without hesitation, he packed his things, and along with his wife, Catherine, left immediately for Washington.

THE KINGDOM OF JACOB

At the time President James Buchanan appointed him secretary of the interior, Jacob Thompson was already one of the most powerful and influential political figures in Mississippi. He held the reins of the Democratic machine and was respected and admired by friends and enemies alike. In northern Mississippi, the First District was his court, and little went on there that Jacob Thompson didn't know about or have a hand in. Like Howry, Dill and Pegues, he was one of Oxford's pioneer citizens who settled Lafayette County in the 1830s, long before there ever was an Oxford. He no doubt had politics on his mind when he first arrived in Pontotoc in 1834, and he quickly established alliances with the most influential political figures in the area. By 1850, he was a wealthy man, a planter and member of Congress who controlled the sociopolitical landscape of northern Mississippi and who had a stake in the continued economic prosperity of the South.

When Thompson first came to the region, it was a raw, wild landscape still inhabited by the Chickasaw Indians. By 1854, the *New and Complete Gazetteer of the United States* described Oxford as:

> *A pleasant and thriving post-village, capital of Lafayette County, Mississippi, 180 miles N. from Jackson. It is considered one of the healthiest places in the state. The state university, which is situated one mile from the village, is well endowed and flourishing, and the buildings are excellent. Oxford has 4 or 5 churches, 2 seminaries for boys, and 2 for girls; 2 newspapers are published here.*

When that description was published, Oxford had only been in existence for seventeen years. Most of the original settlers who came in the 1830s still lived in town and could easily remember when the now thriving community had been a harsh, untamed frontier wilderness, populated only by trappers, squatters, land speculators and bands of roaming Chickasaw Indians. It was the most fertile, richly endowed landscape any of them had ever seen, and they wasted no time in clearing the land, building cabins and planting cotton.

While Jacob Thompson was perhaps the most influential political leader in northern Mississippi, he wasn't by far the first. While many men were responsible for the rapid growth of early Lafayette County, none was more influential than a transplanted South Carolina planter named John Peyton Jones. The development of the county and origins of Oxford are unavoidably the result of Jones's hand in his role as one of the first county commissioners. He was appointed in 1833 by the state to oversee and manage the growth of the region after the Chickasaw Cession, and as cotton became the central motivation for the westward movement to frontier Mississippi, Jones, along with the three other county commissioners, laid out the boundaries, roads and towns like Oxford that would define the region. He was politically connected and widely influential; few things happened in the county that Peyton Jones didn't control.

With an ambition and proclivity toward politics, it seemed inevitable that Jacob Thompson and John Peyton Jones would gravitate toward one another. Like Jones, Thompson came from a wealthy planter family. Tall, gregarious and popular, he was an 1831 graduate of the University of North Carolina at Chapel Hill and by 1834 had earned his law degree. Later that same year, hearing of the newly opened lands along the frontier, he headed west to Pontotoc, the land sales capital of frontier Mississippi. Politically restless and ambitious, he was eager to practice law, surge into politics, acquire land and slaves in the new territory and make his fortune in cotton. As a lawyer, he rode the circuit to small county towns that needed legal services, like Wyatt, College Hill, Paris, Burgess and others. He often stayed over with settlers in their wilderness cabins, and it was on one of these trips that destiny caused his path to cross Jones's. The two men became close friends during the summer of 1835, a friendship that would last the rest of their lives.

But it was not only Jones's powerful political connections and enormous wealth that commanded Thompson's attention. He was also attracted to his beautiful young daughter, Catherine Anne. Kate, as she was called, was a lively, precocious fourteen-year-old when she first met the handsome twenty-five-year-old Thompson in the autumn of 1835. Renowned for her beauty, she was a headstrong girl who had a reputation among the young men for being flirtatious. She enjoyed parties and social intercourse and was known to have had a string of potential suitors after her, despite her young age. One young prospect she may have considered after her move to Mississippi was her next door neighbor on Woodson's Ridge, a twenty-five-year-old bachelor named Alexander Hamilton Pegues. By most accounts, despite his distinguished Huguenot lineage and aristocratic upbringing, Pegues was a disinclined bachelor, as rough and unimproved as the land he lived on, residing in a cabin described by one observer in 1836 as a "rude bachelor affair of logs." Often seen on horseback, Pegues cut a solitary figure riding along the ridge at sunset, surveying his land or hunting with his dogs, accompanied only by his slaves.

In either case, after Thompson came upon the scene, she made it clear that she had found the man she had been looking for. From the outset, Kate and Jacob adored each other; his aristocratic upbringing, political ambitions and his obvious love for Kate must have combined to further seal a permanent alliance between Jones and Thompson, casting together forever the destinies—and fortunes—of the two families. On December 18, 1838, Jacob Thompson married Catherine Ann "Kate" Jones.

Not long after, Alexander Pegues, the bachelor of Woodson's Ridge, also married. He had fallen in love with his cousin, Rebecca Pegues, while on a routine family visit to her home in Dallas County, Alabama. But unlike Jacob and Kate Thompson, theirs was a tumultuous, three-year courtship punctuated by Rebecca's self-deprecation, uncertainty and doubt. "As I told you, I have the highest estimation and regard for you," she wrote the hopeful Alexander in a letter a month after he proposed, but "my feelings are not such as you profess for me." Alexander was crushed. Yet, for the next few years, he was persistent. Finally, in 1844, she had a change of heart, and the two were married on November 25, 1844, settling down on Alexander's plantation on Woodson's Ridge next to Jones's property.

WHEN PROSPERITY REIGNED

The early days on Oxford and Lafayette County were viewed undeniably by most residents as among the happiest and most prosperous in the history of Lafayette County. Once the county and its seat were in place, Oxford and environs grew with the speed of a wildfire. Within three years, the county had grown to 6,531 residents (3,689 whites and 2,842 slaves). Oxford in the 1840s was a very different place than the trendy college town of today. Then, all travel was by horseback, wagon, carriage or on foot. The basic street layout was the same as in modern times, except that streets were unimproved dirt, and when it rained it turned into unimproved mud. Sidewalks consisted of wooden porches and jumbled, irregular plank sidewalks connecting one store to the next. Trade wagons were the main traffic, cutting deep ruts into the square and surrounding roads, their horses leaving souvenir piles for unwary pedestrians to step in and the rain to eventually wash away. Wagon traffic jammed the square; hotels, taverns, liquor shops, law offices, banks, merchant and grocery stores plied their trades—people coming and going in an all-encompassing blur of continuous activity. Liquor was a favorite ingredient to the early town, especially among the university students, who won the reputation for carousing and terrorizing the good people of Oxford with plenty of "drinking and rowdy behavior." Nearly every establishment in town possessed a license to sell or dispense it. Costs for goods and services were average for the day: one could spend the night at the Oxford Inn on the north side of the square for 12 1/2 cents, eat breakfast or dinner for 37 cents and for 12 1/2 cents one could buy a glass of spirits at the end of a long day.

Beneath all the surface busyness and the hustle of commerce there spanned an intricate web of family relationships and close friends, each following the other to Mississippi from all parts of the South. The onrushing migration resembled leaves blowing across a field as brother followed brother, sister followed cousin and father followed son to the Mississippi frontier. The census rolls show proliferations of family names, indicating that whole family groups were transplanted to the area. By 1850, the total population had swollen to 14,065, (8,346 whites and 5,719 slaves), and nearly half the white families in Lafayette County shared the last name with at least one other family. Jacob Thompson's brothers John and William relocated to Oxford, and his brothers-in-law, Will Lewis and Yancey Wiley, also emigrated from North Carolina. The same could be said for the Pegues family, the Bufords, the Dooleys, and many others.

William Smith Neilsen came to Oxford in 1839 from Tennessee and established his first dry goods store in a rough-hewn log cabin located on the northwest corner of what became the courthouse square. A detail-oriented man with a reputation for honesty as a merchant, Neilsen sold a wide selection of wares—from food and groceries, to men's and women's clothing, building supplies, medicines and drugs and even coffins. There was Charles G. Butler who was Lafayette County sheriff and his wife, Burlina, who operated the Oxford Inn. Then there was W.G. Reynolds, whose confectionary shop Rebecca Pegues always took time to patronize with her daughters Eliza and Ella when they came into town. Perhaps as Rebecca left the shop and walked back to her carriage, she might have exchanged greetings with Chancellor Barnard just coming into town, or Judge James Howry walking from the courthouse to the diner, or even Dr. Thomas Isom, the one-time trading post clerk who was now the physician of choice among hosts of prominent families throughout the county.

William Turner was another familiar face, a bachelor living in the household of W.H. Wilkins, minister to the Cumberland Presbyterian Church. With no formal training in carpentry to speak of, he became a well-known builder–contractor in town and was frequently called upon by many of the wealthier families to design and build homes or perform contract work. In 1848, he designed and built a stately Greek-revival home for Colonel Robert Sheegog south of town, the home that became Rowan Oak. Little is known of the Irish-born Sheegog, except that he immigrated to Oxford in the early 1840s and was an affable, well-liked gentleman, a neighbor and friend of the Thompsons, as well as a prominent citizen of the town. On many a moonlit evening before the war came, Colonel Sheegog would have stood on his front porch to enjoy a cigar or two in the quiet cedar and magnolia bemused solitude of his estate. The Thompson home would have been easily seen just across the road beyond his gate, emerging from the distance like a bejeweled bride in all her beauty and magnificence.

The Thompson mansion was, prior to Thomas Pegues's 1859 estate Ammadelle, the most magnificent home in Oxford. It had been a grand undertaking, built by Jacob for Kate and constructed with the finest cut lumber hauled in by wagon from Memphis, its outer walls built of bricks handmade on site by Thompson's own slaves. When it was completed in 1841, Jacob named it Home Place because of its peaceful, domestic setting. Visitors were dazzled by its stately elegance, its sprawling verandas, gardens and a drive lined on both sides by tall cedars. It boasted a caretaker's lodge, a gardener's residence, a carriage house, smokehouse and kitchen and a main house with twenty rooms filled with fine paintings and works of art collected from the Thompson's many travels. Stained-glass windows colored the drawing room, hallways displayed paintings, tapestries and handsome upholsteries. The dining room, which was large enough to seat a hundred guests for dinner, was paneled with imported French mirrors gilded in gold leaf.

By 1856, the Thompson home had become the center of political life in Lafayette County with Jacob its reigning monarch. Governor John J. Pettus and Jefferson Davis were regular guests, the dining room being the stage where the life of sectional political thought played out. It was in that dining room on a June night in 1857 that Thompson sat with the Democratic Party leadership to discuss the nomination of Lucius Lamar for Congress. On that evening, perhaps as he sat looking at his own image in the French mirrors, it must have seemed, at least in Jacob Thompson's own mind, that the stars in his Southern galaxy were now perfectly aligned and following in their proper courses.

CHAPTER 2

CLOSING THE
MISSISSIPPI MIND

"This country has never seen so trying a time during the eight-five years of its history, as is now convulsing it from centre to circumference - from the crowded mart to its most distant outpost."
—R.F. Crenshaw to Miss Ella Austin, December 13, 1860

In 1859, the sectional crisis over slavery and secession that had been playing out on the national stage at last came to Oxford. For some time, residents had been hearing reports and rumors of shadowy outsiders secreting about Lafayette County in an underground movement to destroy slave loyalty and incite rebellion. The newspapers bubbled with reported acts of defiance locally and carried accounts of insurrections in Virginia, Jamaica and elsewhere. The county government ordered that all slaves had to carry passes written by their owners or overseers any time they traveled off the plantation or owner's property. In town, vigilance committees were formed, patrolling the county roads and byways at night, searching for runaways and evidence of unusual activity. A stranger coming into Oxford during this period fell under immediate suspicion of being a Northerner with hidden abolitionist motives.

Fear of slave rebellions on the plantations was omnipresent, and any slave or white man caught inciting an insurrection could be hanged. Yet, such a threat failed to deter some from attempting to meet with slaves under the cover of darkness. Slave owners like Alexander Pegues, who previously encouraged his slaves to read and write, now discouraged it, fearing—like other white planters—that slaves who could read might be in a position to stir up trouble. Groups of slaves standing together were viewed as seedbeds of insurrection. Slaveholders and overseers quickly descended upon such gatherings and broke them up. In outlying parts of Lafayette County, self-styled vigilante groups formed and hunted for whatever they could find, lynching slaves and white men alike simply on suspicion. One of the luckier ones was a man who one day found himself arrested and jailed by Sheriff Butler simply because the locals didn't know him very well. Later that night, an angry mob of townspeople came for him at the jail, dragging him out of the jailhouse and into the dark woods beyond town. Sure he would be lynched, he begged for his life. The mob beat him senseless. Then in a surprising move, they ordered him to "make tracks for yankeedom" and let the man go.

When news of John Brown's slave uprising and raid on the arsenal at Harpers Ferry was heard in Oxford, it horrified an already anxious community and sent fear and paranoia soaring to new heights. It convinced citizens of the genuine threat they faced against abolitionists and Northern fanatics. In the months following, agents of abolition seemed to be behind every bush and tree in Lafayette County. Reports of slave conspiracies on the plantations fed the rumor mill; more vigilante groups were organized and armed after hearing reports of murder and arson among their neighbors. More instances of slave defiance occurred and the number of runaways was on the rise. On a warm, moonless night, a slave of Dudley Isom slipped off his plantation and set fire to neighbor J.M. Dooley's cotton gin. Another slave, suspected of subversive activity, was publicly flogged until he confessed to taking part in an insurrection plot on one of the plantations. Tolerance for such behavior dwindled until it became virtually nonexistent, and many suspects were simply strung up as examples to the rest of the population.

As the paranoia of 1859 spread, few residents trusted anyone they didn't know personally. Strangers who came into town were automatically considered guilty. Once the suspicion was raised, authorities acted swiftly and resolutely. The luckier suspects would be picked up by the sheriff or Vigilance Police and advised they were not welcome, then promptly escorted to the county line and ordered to leave and never return. One such incident involved a man named Simpson and his family who were summarily expelled from the county simply because he kept to himself. No evidence was ever produced against him, yet the *Oxford Intelligencer* warned "there is not a shadow of a doubt that Simpson and his son-in-law are abolitionists." Another account speaks of one of Oxford's own citizens—an unnamed resident who worked as a miller, but who, like Simpson, received a visit from the sheriff and was run out of the county. "Watch him," the Holly Springs newspaper strongly advised, for he was alleged to be in the habit of "going into the woods with negroes" and "reading to them choice passages from the Memphis *Bulletin*." The unluckier suspects were simply apprehended and lynched from a nearby tree by any one of the self-styled vigilante groups.

It was during this period that Oxford came under its own "reign of terror" in which anyone who did not conform to support slavery was considered subversive and either shunned, arrested, exiled or hanged. But the most public display of paranoia and chronic distrust played out on the stage of the University of Mississippi during 1859 and 1860, resulting in the public revilement of its most scholarly and respected chancellor.

THE BRANHAM AFFAIR

Frederick Augustus Porter Barnard came to the University of Mississippi in the fall of 1854 as a professor of mathematics. He was a Northerner, born in Sheffield, Massachusetts, and educated at Yale. Formerly a professor at the University of Alabama, Barnard was a consummate academic and scholar who sought intellectual and moral excellence in everything he did, striving all the while for greater knowledge and spiritual enlightenment. Also an ordained Episcopalian minister, he regularly preached Sundays from the pulpit at St Peter's Episcopalian Church in Oxford, where Alexander and Rebecca Pegues attended. The Pegueses were so impressed with his sermons that Barnard and his wife became close friends and frequent weekend guests at their plantation near College Hill. Pegues was also a trustee of the university, along with Jacob Thompson, James M. Howry, James Brown and Dr. Thomas Isom, all of whom were immediately impressed by Barnard's scholarly attainments. Though not politically inclined, Barnard's friendships with the trustees permitted him to circulate on the fringe of the powerful Southern Democratic political movement, where he became acquainted with many influential Southern politicians, including Mississippi governor Pettus, Lucius Lamar, William Barksdale and Senator Jefferson Davis.

When Augustus B. Longstreet resigned as university president in 1856, Frederick Barnard was immediately chosen as his replacement. Many of Longstreet's friends blamed Barnard's close associations with the trustees as the cause for Longstreet's departure. The actual reason seems to be that Longstreet was incapable of developing the university to the satisfaction of the trustees; this, coupled with his complete inability to control the students

Chancellor Frederick A. Barnard, 1861. While tolerant of slavery and politics, he often complained to his friend E.W. Hilgard of Mississippi's "destructive tendencies." *Courtesy of Special Collections, University of Mississippi Libraries.*

led to his resignation. Now under Barnard, the university's fortunes improved dramatically. The Yale-educated president wanted, more than anything else, to make his University of Mississippi the finest academic institution in the world. He immediately expanded the scientific disciplines and collections, created a graduate program and a law school and even managed to convince the state legislature to appropriate funds so he could build an astronomical observatory on campus, fitted out with what was then the largest telescope in the world.

But his vision of building a great institution was interrupted on a spring night in 1859. Returning home from university business in Vicksburg on the evening of May 12, he learned from Professor E.C. Boynton (who lived in the same faculty house as the Barnards) that someone had broken into his residence and savagely assaulted Barnard's twenty-nine-year-old female house servant named Jane. Boynton told the story how he had heard scuffling and, upon investigation, observed two figures running away in the dark. On his return to his quarters, he discovered Jane, battered and bloodied, lying on the floor. She had been raped and, in defending herself, savagely beaten. Through private inquiries, Boynton later learned the identities of the attackers as two university students, J.P. Furniss and Samuel B. Humphreys.

Barnard was furious. He summoned Humphreys and Furniss before a meeting of the faculty on May 23 to answer to the allegations; both students claimed innocence. Furniss maintained he had taken no part in the attack. But the battered Jane, still bearing visible scars and injuries, positively identified Humphreys as the one who assaulted her. Barnard asked the faculty for Humphreys's immediate dismissal from the university.

The faculty refused. While it did declare Humphreys "morally convicted," it was explained to Barnard that under Mississippi law, slave testimony was inadmissible in proceedings against a white man. As a result, no action was taken against Humphreys.

Barnard walked home that night angry and confused. For all his scholarly attainments and his lofty position as leader of a distinguished institution, he was frustrated and demoralized with the Southern point of view. "The misery of the situation in Mississippi," he wrote in a letter to his close friend, fellow scientist Dr. E.W. Hilgard, "is the destructive tendencies of its people." Such tendencies continued to play out throughout the

Professor E.C. Boynton in 1860. He was a close friend and supporter of Frederick Barnard's efforts to develop the University of Mississippi into a world-class institution. After secession, his Northern sentiments resulted in his arrest and, along with his family, being ignominiously driven out of the state. *Courtesy of Special Collections, University of Mississippi Libraries.*

fall and winter in the form of a whispering campaign, charging that Barnard accepted "negro testimony," and raising the deep suspicion that he was "unsound on the slavery question." This smear campaign was the brainchild of Oxford physician Dr. Henry Branham, a rabid proslavery advocate, son-in-law of former university president August B. Longstreet and brother-in-law to Lucius Lamar. For Branham, it was payback. He hated Barnard without doubt and still held him accountable for Longstreet's humiliating resignation. The rumors not only sullied Barnard's reputation, they created a heated and divisive atmosphere among the faculty, pitting friends and colleagues against one another and "dividing the house." In November, it got even worse as the students were drawn into the controversy. When Barnard again wrote to Hilgard, he expressed his complete disgust. "I would take up any mechanic art," he wrote. "I would even be a private soldier, or a day laborer, before I would again be an officer in a southern college." Finally, when the personal intrigues and rumors against him turned into threats against his life, Barnard wrote to Governor John J. Pettus demanding "the fullest and most searching investigation."

He got his wish. On March 1, 1860, a board of inquiry that included Governor Pettus himself convened in the Lyceum building on campus to hear testimony in the charges that Dr. Branham had publicly filed against Barnard. Seventeen witnesses were called. But the most compelling witness turned out to be Barnard himself. "I was born in the North," he admitted freely and dispassionately. "That I cannot help. I was not consulted in the matter…I am a slave-holder," he said, looking all of them in the eye, "and if I know myself, I am as sound on the slavery question as any member of this board." After a short deliberation, the board of inquiry unanimously absolved him of any suspicion of being "unsound" on slavery, and they published their findings in every newspaper in the state.

That would seem to have been the end of it. But the intrigues and threats continued for a long time after. Disillusioned and depressed, Frederick Barnard set his mind on resigning his position and heading back to Massachusetts. But Jacob Thompson talked him out of it. "I am convinced," he wrote a frustrated Barnard privately, "that you have no cause to fear either personal insult or personal violence from anyone in Oxford…I wish you would go on as you have always done, believing that you have friends who will stand by you." As commencement neared, Barnard agreed to at least stay another year. But he was so worn down by the whole affair that he left Mississippi on a three-month-long scientific expedition with five other astronomers to observe a rare solar eclipse at Cape Chidley peninsula in Labrador, Canada.

The Branham affair had taken its toll on everyone. As if to foreshadow what was to come, the affair caused professors to take sides, polarizing on the slavery issue into either Northern or Southern camps; Professor E.C. Boynton came under permanent scrutiny for his Northern leanings and support of Barnard's slave Jane, eventually becoming the target of yet another smear campaign. For months, Barnard had been suffering from frequent, incapacitating headaches. But now as the steamer headed north toward the Arctic, the headaches disappeared. On nights as the ship slipped northward passed the Newfoundland coast, Barnard delighted in long evenings on deck gazing skyward at the "extensive and very beautiful" displays of the aurora borealis. Suddenly, the world of Oxford, Mississippi, was very far away.

THE LAST HARVEST

The harvest of 1859 was one of the largest and most profitable on record in Lafayette County. It was a bumper crop, producing 19,282 ginned bales of Upland cotton and 644,089 bushels of Indian corn, putting approximately $1.5 million into the pockets of planters and landowners like Alexander Pegues, Jacob Thompson, Lucius Lamar, Yancey Wiley and others. That year, the county ranked twenty-fifth out of sixty counties in the state in output and helped put Mississippi on the map as second only to South Carolina in overall cotton production. By 1860, cotton comprised two-thirds of the total exports of the United States and made up nearly three-quarters of the world's total cotton supply. Mississippi suddenly found itself at the epicenter of the cotton boom, which that year brought to the American market a staggering 535 million pounds. "This is a magnificent country for planters," Augustus B. Longstreet once boasted to his son-in-law, Lucius Lamar in 1850. "There are men here who left Newton County [Georgia] poor and in debt ten years ago, who now have a good plantation and fifteen to twenty hands, and are buying more every year."

That year, Alexander Pegues was the largest landowner in the county. Through discipline, diligent investment and patience, he had more than tripled his property holdings, from a mere 1,520 acres in 1840 to over 5,000 acres of prime cotton land in 1859. His plantation produced 150 bales of ginned cotton worth an estimated $8,085 and 4,000 bushels of corn worth another $3,400 on the open market. His cousin Thomas E. Pegues, who lived near Lafayette Springs, yielded 200 bales, the same as Yancey Wiley (Jacob Thompson's brother-in-law). Pegues and Wiley each made about $10,780 from their cotton alone. Pegues made an additional $5,100 from a 6,000 bushel corn harvest, and Wiley collected $3,400 for his 4,000 bushels of corn. Five other planters also produced record cotton crops: James Bowles with 278 bales, W.T. Avent with 248, T.W. Jones with 235 and W.F. Avent with 202. But the biggest harvest of all went to Jacob Thompson, whose original 2,500 acres on Woodson's Ridge produced a staggering 392 bales of cotton with an approximate market value of $21,000, along with 5,500 bushels of corn worth another $4,675.

As King Cotton thrived, landowners flourished along with it. Planters across the county found themselves suddenly at the height of their wealth and able at last to build the kind of stately homes and lifestyles their aristocratic class permitted. These later plantation homes in Lafayette County were a far cry from the crude, rustic log affairs that defined plantation life during the 1830s and 1840s. Now, suddenly upon the landscape appeared elegant, spacious two-story mansions with lavish, columned fronts, elaborate porticos and sprawling verandas set on well-tended, gardened properties. Even the ramshackle "rude bachelor affair of logs" that had been home to the young Alexander Pegues on Woodson's Ridge, was abandoned and replaced by a more comfortable mansion and accommodations. The glory days of "high cotton" had arrived.

All of it had been possible because of slavery. Behind the elegant facades and ornate porticos, behind the political displays, elected offices and all the rhetoric about Southern honor existed the mighty engine that powered Southern society and the economics of a nation. At the same time, it created a social class that enjoyed an unprecedented level of wealth and privilege, an American caste whose existence depended almost entirely upon the enslavement of the Negro. Had it not been for the invention of the cotton gin in 1793, the institution of slavery would likely have died out in America, and the sectionalist politics that defined the history of early America might never have come to the fore. Civil War would likely never have happened. But the cotton gin allowed more cotton lint to be separated more efficiently

Ammadelle, the Oxford residence of Thomas E.B. Pegues. Built with slave labor in 1859, the elaborate, Italianesque structure is typical of some of the opulent homes wealthy planters of the day created for themselves. Jacob Thompson's Home Place was said to be even more extravagant. *Courtesy of the Library of Congress.*

from the seeds, creating a greater market for cotton and, with it, an increased demand for slaves. Textile industries, especially in Britain, grew dramatically, and slavery became protected within the framework of constitutionality and sustained by political will.

While the word slavery never appears in the Constitution itself, references to it appear in six of its eighty-four clauses, most of them tied to the South's concern over population as the determining factor for representation in Congress. Because the South had a lesser population compared to Northern states, Southern states insisted on concessions as a condition of ratification. Among their responses, the framers of the Constitution included a three-fifths clause that allowed that portion of the slave population to count toward Southern representation. Without the concession, the Constitution would never have been ratified. It can be said that the country owes its very existence, at least in part, to the institution of slavery. It became regulated by the government under strict constitutionality, an economic and political practice that Thomas Jefferson cautioned in 1820 was like holding a wolf by the ears. "We can neither hold him," he maintained, "nor safely let him go. Justice is in one scale, and self-preservation in the other."

"I Don' Kno' Nuthin' but Wurk"

By 1860, there were 7,129 slaves in Lafayette County. Of the 8,889 whites, only 606 were slaveholders, meaning that 7 percent of the white population owned and enslaved 44 percent of the total population of the county. In the town of Oxford itself, there were 368 slaves owned by 67 whites. Slave sales took place either privately between two parties or they could be public, in which case they were conducted on the front steps of the courthouse by Sheriff Charles G. Butler, himself a slaveholder. Slaves were considered valuable commodities and were often sold to pay debts; they were frequently given as gifts and used as deeds of trust. Runaways that were caught were kept in the jail, where they languished sometimes for months, while advertisements were posted in the newspaper for the owner to come forward, pay the fees and claim his property. Under Mississippi law, a slave was considered a runaway if he or she was more than eight miles from their domicile without written authorization. Slaves that were not claimed went to one of Butler's public auctions. Burlina W. Butler, owner of the Oxford Inn on the square, owned 12 slaves, the majority being domestic females between the ages of twelve and fourteen. Merchant William Smith Neilsen was the master of 9 slaves

State of Miss[iss]pp[i]
Lafayette c[ounty]

Rec[eive]d of A H Pegues
One thousand dollars for a negro woman
named Susan of dark complexion
& about 18 years of age. I warrant her
sound in body & mind, a Slave for life
& title good. Dec= 25 th 1850
Joseph Hickey

Receipt from Joseph Hickey of Oxford for the private sale of an eighteen-year-old slave named Susan, bought for one thousand dollars by Alexander Pegues on Christmas Day 1850. *Courtesy of Special Collections, University of Mississippi Libraries.*

and gained a reputation as a kind and paternalistic owner. Dr. Thomas Isom owned 7 slaves; Judge James Howry, 11; builder William Turner, 7; Robert Sheegog, 8; and W.G. Reynolds, whose popular confectionary shop on the square Rebecca Pegues often visited with her girls on trips to town, owned 8 slaves, all children but one.

Slaves were divided into several groups. House servants were considered a select corps of workers, followed by skilled property servants who cared for the house, its grounds, carriages and horses. A middle group of black slave drivers were the top echelon of the plantation slaves, followed by skilled craftsmen, such as carpenters, blacksmiths and bricklayers, and finally a lower class of unskilled fieldworkers, whose job it was to plow, plant, pick and chop cotton. During cultivating months, life was one continuous blur of activity to and from the fields: land had to be cleared of timber, stumps removed and earth plowed to prepare for planting. There were barns and sheds to be built for grain, plows and implements to fix, wagons and machinery to be repaired and cotton to be picked, ginned and baled for market. There was corn to be shelled, hogs to be butchered, bacon and sausage to be made, thread to be spun and cloth to be woven. All of it was done with hands and backs and legs and sweat, and the work never stopped.

Fields were plowed in March or April, planting was done in early May. By the middle of September, the cotton was ready for picking along with corn and other crops. Controlling everything was the overseer—a white man entrusted with running the day-to-day operations and who saw to it that work got done on time, order was maintained and the highest profits possible were achieved for the landowner. Slaves reported early each morning for work in the fields and their names were recorded in a book kept by the overseer. Then a black slave driver led them off in procession to the fields, and when they returned that night, they were again counted. Plantation slaves labored all day without reprieve—bending and turning, fingers bleeding, hauling baskets or duck cloth slings laden with freshly picked cotton or grain. As they worked, small groups might sometimes break into mournful chants to make the time go by or to deaden the monotony.

For slaves like Lucindy Hall Shaw, work began at sunup and continued until after sundown. "I had to wurk mity hard," she later recalled years after the war. "I had to plow in de fiel's in de day an den at nite when I wuz so tired I cu'dn't hardly stan." Lucindy was eleven in 1860 and was owned by Reuben T. Hall and his wife, Sarah, one of the many yeoman farmers who struggled to make enough to get by. Besides Lucindy, the Halls owned three

Slave cabins similar to those that existed on many of the larger Lafayette County plantations. *Courtesy of the Library of Congress.*

other slaves, all of whom slept on the kitchen floor under "one quilt an' kivver." If a slave owner was harsh, slaves sometimes protested by slowing down work, breaking tools and implements, claiming ignorance or causing disturbances among the slave population that took the overseer's time and tried his patience. The most rebellious ones simply ran off.

By October 1860, runaway slaves had become a worrisome problem in Lafayette County, enough so that the Agricultural Association drafted a codified set of "suitable rules for the more strict governance of negroes." The slave code, as it was called, limited the movement of slaves and confined them to the properties of their owners. It also required any slave that left the property to have in their possession written permission from the owner or overseer. The code prohibited any slave from coming into Oxford itself, from buying or selling, and it imposed a ten o'clock curfew countywide. Slave owners were required to personally visit their slave cabins, count their slaves and report the missing. A "paid police" was organized to patrol the county and enforce order. "Sometimes de houses wu'd be full of patrollers lukin' fer slaves dat run away," remembered Lucindy. Polly Turner Cancer, one of William Turner's slaves recalled, "We allus had a git a pass to travel 'round at night. Dat's what dey kep de patrollers fur; to keep de niggers frum runnin' 'round at nite an' frum runnin' away."

Lafayette County plantations with large slave populations often became incubators for disease, especially after the fall harvests when the cold weather set in. Everyone dreaded winter months, when illness could indiscriminately fell slave and master alike. "I have been trembling all day with anxiety— so much afraid I would hear of more sickness," confided Rebecca Pegues to her diary. Disease and death was a universal physical fear in 1860. When one became sick, medicines did little to relieve the misery. Typhoid, pneumonia, influenza and dysentery were the most common afflictions to infect plantation populations. Among the slaves, they were especially lethal to children. Sometimes prayer was the only thing that gave comfort to a victim before the inevitability of death overcame them.

Some Lafayette County slave owners went to lengths to improve the lives of their slaves. "Miss Betsy tried to teach me to read and write," remembered "Aunt Jane" McLeod Wilburn years afterward. Jane was born in Lafayette Springs and was owned by Angus and Betsy McLeod of Oxford. She was bought from a man named Scrivener of Grenada and became the McLeods' house servant and nurse to their children. "I wud study at nite, when I wuzn't playing wid de white chillum…I've always had good white folks, an' been taken keer uv all my life." Polly Cancer remembered her master, "Marst Bill," as a "funny, good ole man" who made sure his slaves were taken care of and well fed. "When we wuz sick ole Miss looked atter us; if we wuz sick she'd have us put on a trundle bed an' wait on us nite an' day til we got well."

At the other end of the scale was the experience of Lucindy Hall Shaw. More than seventy years after the end of the Civil War and freedom, she had no fondness whatsoever for her former owners. "Dey ust to beat me lak I wuz a dog; de white folks'd beat me an' de cullered folks 'ud beat me de same as de white folks." Pain and death was an everyday reality that hung over the lives of every slave. Lucindy remembered in chilling detail witnessing the brutal murder of a slave mother and her aborted baby as she was tied to a tree and flogged to death by the overseer before her eyes. "Dey entied her an' she wuz de'd," Lucindy recalled. "Dey jus' called an' old grandpap slave 'round...an' dug her gravesite dar. I sez grave, but it wuzn't nuthin' but a hole in de groun'. He tok de shovel an' jus' rolled her in, an' den he shoveled in sumthin'...I tho't I saw move. I tell Miss Sarah, but she 'tend lak she didn't see nuthin'. She w'udn't tell me den but she tol' me atterwards, dat de overseer whipped her so hard she birfed a baby."

While slaves constituted valuable property, slave killing in Lafayette County was not unknown. In one notorious case in 1859, wealthy local landowner George Oliver killed his slave John after an argument over the slave's refusal to give up a tool called a punch, which was used in a corn shelling machine. Oliver testified that after repeated

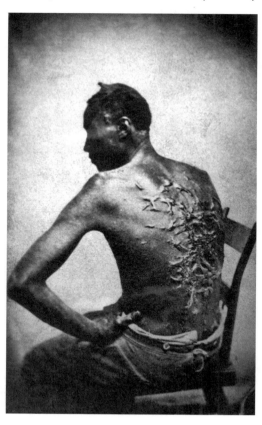

Runaways and troublesome slaves were often dealt with harshly, as in the case of this man. *Courtesy of the Library of Congress.*

refusals to give up the tool, he wrestled it away from John (described as a "very stout and strong man") and repeatedly struck him over the head until the slave fell dead. At Oliver's trial, his overseer, a man named Bramwel, testified that Oliver killed John "for nothing." The evidence against him must have been conclusive, because the state won a conviction against Oliver for manslaughter. Robert Stowers, an overseer for Jacob Thompson, acquired a broad reputation for being able to break troublesome slaves. He was so good at it that owners from other plantations would send their most difficult slaves to be "corrected." Stowers used the method of whipping and then "salting"—a common practice of the day in which salt, and sometimes pepper, was rubbed into wounds to increase the pain. One former slave said that Stowers always carried a shovel with him wherever he went "to bury de niggers after he killed 'em."

It would not be long, however, before all that would change.

TRIUMPH OF THE FIRE-EATERS

On the morning of May 5, 1860, Alexander Pegues, who by then was a Mississippi state senator and electioneer, arrived in Charleston to meet with the delegates of the Democratic National Convention. He had come at the request of Secretary of the Interior Jacob Thompson and other party heavyweights to help restore some kind of order to the proceedings. The convention was in serious trouble. For two weeks, delegations bickered and fought over sectionalist sentiments as they attempted to select a nominee for the upcoming presidential election. On the convention floor, Pegues encountered a frustrated Lucius Lamar and Jacob Thompson. The situation, they said, was desperate. Sectional politics within the party had caused the splintering of delegations into irreconcilable factions that threatened the ability of the party to put forward any kind of a credible nominee for president. In so doing, Thompson believed, the delegates subjected themselves to misrepresentation and denunciation of their own principles. "As soon as the Democratic Party ceases to be the party of the Constitution and the Union," he wrote on May 23 to a Democratic gathering in Memphis, "it should be dissolved; it ought not to outlive its principles."

The Southern extremist movement had received its formal incarnation only three months earlier in the form of six resolutions introduced in Congress by Senator Jefferson Davis. The Davis Resolutions were an attempt to unify a party that was slowly destroying itself from within. They were an amalgam of years of Democratic Party thought forged into a cohesive position intended to represent mainstream party policy. Among the provisions, Davis maintained that no state could interfere with another state's internal affairs; that an attack on slavery was a violation of the Constitution; that Congress should be forbidden from impairing the right of any state or territory to hold slaves; and, finally, that the recovery of fugitive slaves was to remain a constitutional right.

For three years, Lucius Lamar had assailed Washington in his own right as a Mississippi congressional representative and voice of crisis; now he was in Charleston at the behest of Davis to deliver a message that the party must remain united at all costs in defeating Stephen A. Douglas and his "popular sovereignty" platform. The dutiful Lamar delivered Davis's message to the convention from the podium, then along with Pegues and Thompson, circulated and harangued groups of delegates for hours. It did little good. At the end of the night, the Mississippi delegation simply stormed out in disgust. Delegates from the other states were right behind them. The Democratic National Convention adjourned in complete chaos.

In Washington, Jefferson Davis was appalled. In an effort to mitigate the damage, he and other leaders signed and circulated a petition to all Democrats to reconvene for another convention in Baltimore. Most delegates simply ignored him. But Lamar, probably out of loyalty to Davis rather than of his own conviction, put his signature next to Davis's, then turned his eyes toward Baltimore. "Davis had signed it," he later explained in a letter to his old law partner Christopher H. Mott, "and I was determined that his name should not go unsupported by any of the delegation." With the party still in disarray, the Southern Democrats managed to meet in Baltimore and nominate Kentuckian John C. Breckinridge as their candidate, while the Northern faction of the party nominated Stephen A. Douglas at their convention in Richmond.

Back in Oxford, the citizens were ready for blood. Jefferson Davis came to town on September 26 with Lucius Lamar and addressed the people from the steps of the courthouse. "We have a common enemy," he began, "and must share a common fate." He spoke for over two hours to a large audience that packed the square, with a voice thin, hoarse and tired, but it stirred the audience until frenzied fists were raised and loud shouts of defiance rang out. He reminded them how Abraham Lincoln had declared that there was an irrepressible conflict between freedom and slavery. "This doctrine is," Davis emphasized, "as against the South, a declaration of perpetual war." Governor Pettus also came to Oxford with forebodings

Senator Jefferson Davis became the defining figure in the struggle for Southern identity. Despite pride in his long record of military and political service to the Union, "I was still more proud of the fact that I was a son of Mississippi." *Courtesy of the Library of Congress.*

of what was to come. "The next compromise we offer, and the next demand we make," he regaled from the courthouse steps, his hands held as if firing a rifle, "will be with our guns leveled at the breasts of the unfeeling tyrants and saying—we fight, we die, but we yield no more!" Congressman Reuben Davis further warned his constituents that the road they were now going down was likely to be a bloody one. "We will resist!" he declared. "We will sacrifice our lives...and convert our sunny South... into a wilderness waste...we will be butchered first!"

But the overall mood of Lafayette County was perhaps best summed up in an editorial in the November 21, 1860 edition of the *Oxford Intelligencer*:

We have endured wrong and insult from the abolition fanatics, until endurance has ceased to be a virtue...we must at once, promptly, unhesitatingly, and dispassionately, withdraw ourselves from the influence and power of Abolitionism, the deadly upas tree that has shed a poisoning blight upon the happiness of this once glorious Union.

On her plantation near College Hill, Rebecca Pegues sat at her table and confided to her diary, "We are in the beginning of a revolution."

CHAPTER 3

THE IMPRISONED WINDS ARE LET LOOSE

"So strongly am I attached to the Union, that, to retain its blessings I would surrender anything except those rights which cannot be yielded up without dishonor."
—*Senator Jefferson Davis, September 26, 1860*

When the election of Abraham Lincoln became a certainty, it signaled to the Southern states that the discussion over slavery and secession had entered a new phase. The time for debate had passed; there would be no more compromises. Southern politicians could no longer deny that events within the Union had become an irreconcilable rupture between North and South, one that boiled and seethed with hostility as it had against the British in the days of the American Revolution. Now another revolution was upon them, and the citizens of Lafayette County were heading down a road whose path they did not know, whose glories they could see adorning its roadside like a bride in her jewels, but whose end was as yet unknown and beyond the horizon of their comprehension.

To most Southerners, the election of the Illinois Rail-Splitter had been a Northern plot. Out of thirty-three states in the Union, Lincoln did not even appear on the ballots of ten Southern states; South Carolina did not even participate in the election of 1860. Yet Lincoln still managed to beat Stephen A. Douglas, John Breckinridge and John Bell by a substantial margin. The outcome only served to confirm what was viewed in Mississippi as a conspiracy by the North in furthering their "avowed opposition to the vital institutions of the South." Now, for the first time in history, there was in both the Congress and in the executive branch a majority rule by a political party established almost entirely on the sectional issue of slavery. The Republicans became known as the Black Republicans, and Lincoln became the hated face of abolition itself, the author of the saying that a nation "cannot remain half slave and half free," the man whom Southerners believed all along, if elected, would wage war against their economic and social system by abolishing slavery. He now had the position, the means and the political support to do it. The spirit of openness in the South—if it ever existed after 1850—disappeared forever with the election of 1860, and left the people of the Southern states with the only option left to them: secession.

Five days after the election, an anxious and dejected Lucius Lamar wrote to his father-in-law, Augustus Longstreet in Oxford: "If South Carolina will only have the courage to go out, all will be well. We will have a Southern Republic, or an amended Federal Constitution that will place our institutions beyond the attack in the future." Lamar's view that a peaceful solution was

President-elect Abraham Lincoln after the election of 1860. The suddenness of secession took even Lincoln by surprise. As Southern states fell, he continued to insist that the federal government had "both the authority and the power to maintain its own integrity." *Courtesy of the Library of Congress.*

still at least feasible hung in his thoughts for some time, even as half the country careened toward secession. No one, least of all Lamar, could be certain of the outcome. But the South by then had begun to take matters into its own hands. In Lafayette County, discussion among the political leaders about what to do ensued in earnest. What will Mississippi's answer be to the election of the Black Republican Lincoln?

Jacob Thompson, Lucius Lamar, Alexander Pegues and the political leadership of Lafayette County now contemplated their fate. As they did so, it must have seemed that the voices of the founding fathers were speaking to them from the past, words that came rushing back before them like a shimmering vision, showing them the unalterable path they must tread if they are to be true to the constitutional principles they so passionately professed. Suddenly, they saw their efforts fueled by the same determination and convictions that once had compelled Jefferson and Washington to rebel against their British oppressors, and in their minds they again heard the sacred words "life, liberty, and the pursuit of happiness" along with the stern reminder that "whenever any form of government becomes destructive to these ends, it is the right of the people to alter or to abolish it, and to institute new government."

Now a kind of patriotism in the spirit of the American Revolution swept through Oxford like a strong wind. The "Spirit of '76" now became the "Spirit of '61," and its rebellious influence was felt everywhere. Crowds gathered in the courthouse square, bands played, patriotic speeches echoed off the buildings, church bells pealed, guns fired into the air, banners sewn by young ladies for their young men fluttered in the breezes and cockades made of red, white and blue ribbon decorated hats, lapels, dresses and coats. The spirit soon evolved into a reincarnation of the American Revolution itself, a frenzied loyalty to the very principles of the founding fathers as they saw them expressed in the Constitution.

"The cause" was born. Its tenet bound each citizen of the South together in unity and compelled them, as the British once compelled their colonies, to break away and war for independence. Political leaders no longer had to worry about how to sell secession to the public. Newspapers, like Howard Falconer's weekly *Oxford Intelligencer*, published a steady stream of articles explaining in agonizing detail the constitutional righteousness of the cause of secession. "The citizens of a State have a perfect right to secede from the Union," wrote the *Mississippian*, "whenever a majority, through a convention, decides that they have sufficient right." The *Natchez Free Trader* insisted on "immediate secession or submission," while the *Vicksburg Sun* declared that

Mississippi could not submit to Lincoln without "dishonor and degradation." On November 21, the *Natchez Courier* quotes the *Oxford Mercury* as saying, "Calmly and dispassionately we raise a voice for a Southern Confederacy… The Union was formed for the common interests and the common safety and protection of all the states. Now it is on the eve of passing into the hands of Abraham Lincoln, a course, illiterate, low-born scoundrel; and Hannibal Hamlin, a man whose blood is one half negro, who intends to pervert it for the oppression and annihilation of the South." Remarking on the trend of other states toward secession, the *Intelligencer* printed, "Let them be united in going out of a Union which refuses them equality." Yet not everyone sided with the mainstream view. The *Vicksburg Whig*, a conservative newspaper, advocated resistance but not secession. "As for us," it concluded, "we will stand by the Union, the Constitution, and the Laws!"

On November 24, 1860, a meeting convened in the Oxford courthouse chaired by H.A. Barr, with Alexander Pegues and K. Houseman presiding. Unlike the fiery rhetoric that set the tempo for the election, this was a solemn and politically neutral gathering intended to "give expression to the opinions and sentiments of the people of Lafayette County in regard to the election of Lincoln and Hamlin." A bipartisan committee was appointed that included Alexander Pegues, his cousin Thomas E.B. Pegues, Dr. Thomas Dudley Isom and four other prominent citizens who drafted a number of resolutions as to the course of action the town should take. Read to the gathering by Alexander Pegues, the resolutions concluded that the election of the Black Republicans to power "indicates a settled and fixed hostility on the part of the people of the Northern States…It is the imperative duty of the slaveholding states to resist and repel encroachments upon their constitutional rights…for the preservation and perpetuity of their peculiar institutions, and the security and safety of the lives, property and just rights of their citizens." The committee also called for a "state convention…to determine the attitude which Mississippi shall assume in the present alarming state of our federal relations."

In Washington, Jacob Thompson began to calculate the precariousness of his own state of affairs. His time as secretary of the interior to President James Buchanan was coming to its predictable close. But now, the coming of Lincoln and the troublesome state of agitation it plunged the country into caused a noticeable shift in relations throughout Washington society. Suddenly the crystal galas and elegant, hoop-skirted balls with the polite, flowery conversation became less frequent and more somber; now all people could talk about was the coming war and the inevitable end to old friendships.

Jacob and Kate Thompson, along with their niece Sallie Wiley (who was living with them in Washington), had become close friends with President Buchanan and his niece, Harriet Lane, who was the White House hostess. Now Buchanan was more distant and reserved. Earlier that year, he had begun a program of spying and intelligence gathering against the Southern states and their diplomats to help him measure the state of the growing crisis. Thompson became one of the Southerners Buchanan now watched.

As a rainy November turned into a cold December, Mississippi's leaders in Jackson sought passage of immediate secession resolutions. Lucius Lamar, who once dabbled with the notion of seeking Southern rights within "an amended Federal Constitution," now abandoned the idea and never considered it again. From that point on, he was bound to cast his lot with the destiny of his state and would follow its fortunes wherever he was led. Meanwhile, Jacob Thompson became ever more alarmed about the chasm that continued to widen between North and South, and he became convinced there was little hope of saving the country, that with the election of Lincoln (whom he once called an "inept blunderer") the only recourse left to settle their differences was civil war. The prospect frightened him. "If… blind devotion to the fortunes of a favorite, or fear to join in the general issue with the Black Republican party of the North, shall rule the hour," he wrote to party members in Memphis, "the day is lost before the battle is begun."

THOSE WHOM GOD WISHES TO DESTROY, HE FIRST MAKES MAD

On a cold December morning in 1860, Oxford residents awoke to the news that South Carolina at last had seceded from the Union. With South Carolina out, other Southern states were sure to follow. It was now impossible to turn back the tide that was sweeping them all down the road toward separation. Jackson's *Weekly Mississippian* proposed immediate secession as the "only path of honor and of safety." In its editorial, it declared, "Let the final act of secession be taken and fully consummated while the Federal Government is in friendly hands…Delay is dangerous. Now is the time to strike. Let not a moment be lost." Conventions in other states began to organize and meet, showing their constitutional resolve to the North one last time by demanding "their full rights under the Constitution, not more, nor less."

While Lucius Lamar was convinced secession was the only path available, Secretary of the Interior Jacob Thompson, watching the drama unfold from his Washington hotel, still wanted to believe, perhaps naively, that there was a possibility of salvaging the situation. Even as a slaveholder and ardent proponent of Southern rights, he did not always support secession, a proposition he felt would bring economic disaster and war. While there was talk in the nation's capital of a possible compromise being hammered out, few believed it. There was no Henry Clay this time to mend the national fabric with an eleventh-hour compromise as he had in 1850. Senators and representatives simply closed their offices, packed their things and left Washington without looking back. Secession, Thompson came to realize, was the narcotic of the disenchanted.

Yet, some weren't ready to give up entirely on attempts to stem secession's tide. With less than two months to go in federal office, Thompson wrote to Buchanan detailing his own ideas about the present crisis and suggesting how either he or Lincoln might resolve it. He proposed that the federal government at least acknowledge the most fundamental rights of the Southern states and allow those states the right of self-determination. He also proposed, as a goodwill gesture, evacuating federal forts in the South as a measure to defuse any militant responses and thus avoid conflict. Meanwhile, Buchanan's intelligence already confirmed the South was actively mobilizing for war with great rapidity. In his message to Congress on December 3, Buchanan spoke directly to the South. He formally recognized the grievances of the Southern states, criticized the interference by the federal government in Southern affairs, but he went on to say that the federal government was unable to prevent secession by military means and appealed to the already seceded states to reconsider their position. He proposed a constitutional amendment that "would forever terminate the existing dimensions and restore peace and harmony among the states." The South simply ignored him. Even if the slavery question could be settled by amendment, the newspapers replied, it "would still leave the North in undisputed possession of all the powers of the general government."

On December 18, in a conciliatory move, Kentucky senator John J. Crittenden introduced a resolution recognizing slavery in all U.S. territories south of N 36°30'. A Senate committee reviewed the Crittenden resolution and unanimously approved it on December 31. Lincoln, however, would not even consider it. On February 4, a peace convention called by the Virginia assembly and chaired by former president John Tyler met in Washington along with representatives from Northern, border and Southern states. When the convention at last summoned Lincoln for a frank exchange of views, no agreement could be reached. "I feared that the blunderer Lincoln would turn and adopt my ideas of states rights," wrote an angry Jacob Thompson in a letter to Buchanan six months later. "Had he done so, secession would have been killed off forever." Frustrated and depressed, Thompson knew it was all or nothing. From then on, rather than see any secession ordinance nullified and his state return to her former position in the old Union, he preferred to see Mississippi "with all her brave sons and fair daughters, and her rich fields, sunk to the bottom of the deep sea, and her name blotted from the map of the earth forever."

In the Midst of Stirring Times

As peace overtures stalled in Washington, events now began to happen quickly in the South. In Mississippi at least, leaving the Union was not a simple matter. Secession was a serious endeavor that required an ordered legislative process, regulated and officiated over and adhering to strict parliamentary protocols. After all, these were turbulent waters the political leadership now sailed. Secession had never been tried before, and despite the prevailing confidence and revolutionary fervor, what was going to happen next was anything but clear. The more seasoned political heads knew that even stormier waters waited just beyond the horizon, and while the revolution was winding up outside the courthouse with the sounds of church bells, band music and pistol shots, inside, at least, cooler heads needed to prevail.

On December 20, a large crowd gathered in the courthouse to select two delegates to represent the county at the upcoming Secession Convention in Jackson. Lucius Lamar, Lafayette County's favorite fire-eater, was quickly chosen as a delegate. The other man chosen with him for the convention ticket was his old friend, the familiar Dr. Thomas Dudley Isom, a well-known pioneer citizen of Oxford and respected pillar of the community. Unlike the colorful Lamar, Isom was a former conservative Whig with no real political experience. Thoughtful and moderate in his politics, he had been opposed to secession except as a last resort. But he was a landowner with slaves and that made him a safe choice. The selection of Isom seems to have been an effort by the committee to balance the ticket—to be fair, if you will—to lend some degree of patronage perhaps to any small minority who held an opposite view and opposed secession. On January 7, the Secession Convention opened in the state Capitol with Lamar and Isom in attendance.

Meanwhile back in Washington, Jacob Thompson sat down to dinner one evening but could not eat. It had been nearly four years since he came to

Washington as part of Buchanan's cabinet. He and Kate had always enjoyed the fast pace of Washington society—the balls, the galas, the political pomp and the bonds of friendship they had made, some of which went as far back as 1839 to Thompson's first term in Congress. He no doubt hoped it would all continue. But he was fifty-one years old now—the same age as Lincoln—and he was supposed to be reaching the peak of his political career. Instead, his political world was unraveling, and he had been advised secretly that Mississippi would soon follow South Carolina out of the Union. He expressed his concerns to Kate and his niece Sallie over dinner and solicited their opinions about the whole state of affairs. Then he proposed they leave for home as soon as possible. On January 8, Jacob Thompson laid his letter of resignation on the desk of President Buchanan and departed for Oxford.

The next day, Mississippi seceded from the Union.

WE BAND OF BROTHERS

In the following weeks and months, a new wave of patriotic militarism swept over Lafayette County. With the Buchanan administration now a lame duck, the assumption of Lincoln and the Black Republicans to power was a reality. Everyone on both sides knew that war was coming, and they began to prepare for it in earnest. Efforts to mobilize a military began at home where patriotism was the most valued. In Oxford, the courthouse square became the stage upon which all the high drama of patriotic display was performed. Military units were formed in anticipation of the coming conflict. Groups like the Avent Southrons and Pegues Defenders were organized, financed entirely by the wealthy planters whose names they bore. Other units formed, too: the Lafayette Dragoons, Jeff Davis Rifles, the Home Guards, McClung Riflemen and the Lafayette Guards, funded almost entirely by the county's wealthy planters. William S. Neilsen, one of Oxford's pioneer citizens, although too old to go to war, did his part by outfitting a number of companies with goods from his mercantile business. When his son and nephew eventually enlisted, he gave each of them a personal body servant to take along.

Women throughout the county played a critical role in supporting the mobilization by making and sewing uniforms, creating regimental flags and banners, feeding and sustaining hungry young men and designing the patriotic cockades for the lapels and hats of their uniformed patriots. Rebecca Pegues led the effort by organizing the Ladies Society into a sewing group that met several times a week to sew for the various military companies.

Other patriotic ladies from the community pitched in, staging charity events to support the soldiers. Private citizens contributed what they could to outfit troops with uniforms, swords, pistols and saddles. Even small girls and young ladies darned socks and shirts for their beaus, and wives sewed their husbands' first uniforms. "When lovely women not only smile upon our efforts to maintain our rights, but lends also a helping hand to the good work," one newspaper wrote, "who can doubt our conquering in the fight?"

One of the more prominent military companies to organize was the Lamar Rifles, named in honor of Congressman L.Q.C. Lamar and captained by thirty-six-year-old Oxford lawyer Francis M. Green. The company was quick to sign on recruits, nearly all of whom were the sons of wealthy planters and professional men with a small mix of university students. The muster roll read like a who's who of Oxford's planter society, among them Second Corporal James H. Howry, son of Judge James Howry; Private Charles B. Neilsen, son of merchant William Neilsen; Private Thomas P. Buford, Goodlow's son; and Lieutenant James Sheegog, son of Robert Sheegog, the neighbor of Jacob Thompson.

The other company that rose to prominence early on was a group composed almost entirely of university students. The University Greys, as it came to be called, were formed not in Oxford's courthouse square but on the campus of the University of Mississippi, the inspiration of a domineering nineteen-year-old law student named William B. Lowry. Ever since secession, the students seethed with a frenzied patriotic energy, and Lowry, who had once attended military school, seized upon the opportunity to create a company of his own that he could drill, mold and command. The students quickly recognized Lowry's leadership skills and elected him their captain. They were a roughshod bunch at first, marching in civilian attire and wielding broom handles for weapons. But Lowry drilled them and made them into at least a demonstrable group. "They proudly paraded the streets of Oxford as soldiers ready to do the bidding of their state," wrote the *Weekly Clarion*. "Watch and wait for the coming of the hour when they could illustrate their patriotism by deeds of valor."

For months, Lowry prowled the campus dormitories and appealed to his college classmates to come join his company and partake in the great adventure that awaited them. One by one they came, either out of a sense of patriotism or perhaps out of a sense of embarrassment to themselves and their families if they did not go. In all, Lowry managed to enlist seventy-five men into the company—forty-two of them students, thirty-three from the county. Among the students to enlist were Henderson Jacobway, Thomas

University of Mississippi law student Jeremiah Gage was typical of the students who followed William Lowry off to war. Here he posed for a graduation snapshot in the summer of 1859, full of optimism and proudly wearing his fraternity pin. *Courtesy of Special Collections, University of Mississippi Libraries.*

B. Tucker, Willis Lea, William Etheridge and a young law student named Jeremiah Gage. Also among their ranks from the county were Samuel M. Brewer, George M. Moseley, Parmeno Harding and Levins Bisland. By April, they had become a close-knit band of brothers, soldiers ready to go fight for their Confederacy. All they wanted now was the chance to prove it.

But to the university faculty, they were still just college kids who were now neglecting their studies in lieu of immersing themselves in the patriotic fervor by drilling with Lowry. Of greatest concern to the faculty was William Lowry himself. He had a long history with the university as a troublemaker. The faculty minutes record repeated disciplinary problems, one involving a fight with a fellow student named Slack and for "having more than fifty marks for absence from College exercises" that caused repeated dismissals. Yet, Lowry made the University Greys what they were and what they became, and his company followed him in spite of his reputation. Despite Chancellor

Barnard's objections, Governor Pettus and the Mississippi legislature eventually granted the University Greys their commissions, making them eligible for state service. Finally, General Griffith came to Oxford in late February to muster in the Lamar Rifles, University Greys and the Lafayette Guards. Howard Falconer, editor of the *Intelligencer*, stated that "Oxford is the banner town of the state, giving to her three companies in one day." They all entered Confederate service on February 22, 1861, as part of the state militia forces. They were now as one observer put it, Mississippi's "buds of promise in the field and forum."

On March 9, the Lamar Rifles received their company flag from the ladies of Oxford. Two companies from Holly Springs came down on the train and were met at the depot by the Lamar Rifles, who greeted them with a volley of musketry. They marched back to University Hotel, enjoyed a sumptuous banquet and then adjourned to the Cumberland Presbyterian Church along with a crowd of several hundred citizens. The *Oxford Mercury* for March 14 gives a detailed description of the presentation. Seven young ladies of the town dressed in snowy white gowns with powder blue sashes (gilt with the names of each seceded state) gracefully moved down the right aisle of the standing-room-only church toward the stage at the front. Representing Mississippi was Sallie Wiley, Yancey Wiley's daughter and a niece of Jacob Thompson. She was escorted by Captain Green up the aisle and onto the platform. A woman who was there as a young girl remembered years later how the plumes on the captain's hat brushed the chandeliers as he marched under them, causing the prisms to jingle. In presenting the flag to Captain Green, Sallie Wiley afterward encapsulated the sentiments of a people who now looked to the young men who would go off to war. "When that hour comes," she said in her speech before the congregation, "we rely upon your strong arms and unquailing hearts to defend our rights, defend the mothers, shield the honor of the maidens of the land, and give security and peace to our firesides."

Throughout March and into April, dinners, parties, concerts and ceremonies became the norm as each company drilled and prepared to go off to the glorious fight. One event, remembered by Chancellor Barnard in a letter to his good friend Dr. E.W. Hilgard, occurred on the evening of Friday, April 5. Upon the square in front of the courthouse were assembled a stage and chairs for a concert to be given by a group of young ladies in Oxford honoring the University Greys. It was a cool, moonless evening with most of the leaders of the town in attendance. Chancellor and Mrs. Barnard sat between Jacob and Kate Thompson and Lucius and Virginia Lamar. As the young ladies presented their renditions of patriotic songs and speeches, Barnard, who was close to the Thompsons, was amused by all of it, and apparently wondered how this sort of patriotic display compared to what they were used to in Washington. "The performance—*risum teneatis amici*—I can't describe it," he wrote in a letter to Hilgard. "But everybody assumed it was good." Barnard leaned over to Mrs. Thompson and smiled politely. "If you *make believe* a good deal," he suggested to her, "I suppose it is very much like Washington." "Yes," she replied, smiling back in agreement. "If you make believe *a good deal!*"

But a Federal fort on a small island out in Charleston harbor would soon bring an end to all the pleasantries. "Fort Sumter is ours!" wrote the *Intelligencer*'s new editor, Francis Duval, who replaced Howard Falconer after he enlisted to go off and fight. "We have long believed that war was inevitable." Lincoln's proclamation calling for seventy-five thousand volunteers for the war was also printed. Oxford celebrated the news that evening with continuous cannon fire from the town's big seven pounder. In their zeal, the artillerymen overloaded the powder charge on more than one occasion, and on the following morning, the windows of the shops on the south side of the square looked "as if they had been through the wars." When Virginia seceded on April 17, the cannon was fired again, with similar results. In the May 1 issue of the *Intelligencer* appeared a notice saying, "We think it best, hereafter, not to fire the cannon in any more salutes. Let us save the powder we have to send balls and grapeshot to the enemy." A week later, the waiting game was over as the Lamar Rifles and the University Greys received word they would soon be heading off to the front.

It was Wednesday, May 1 when they left, a sunny and cloudless morning as friends and relatives gathered at the Oxford depot under a blue sky to bid their farewells. The companies marched in full gear from their armories in town down Depot Street, looking every inch like an undulating serpent in perfect rhythm to the band that led them, their new bayonets glistening in the sunlight. As the formalities got underway, Jacob Thompson mounted the platform and said a few parting words, along with Lucius Lamar, who gave the prophetic warning, "I believe you will see hard service and serious work." But the time of high spirits and speeches soon ended and the rushed, final goodbyes were said as the call for boarding went out. Captain Francis Green, one of only four married soldiers in the Lamar Rifles, and Private James O'Grady, the only married member of the University Greys, both stood locked in long, lasting embraces and intimate farewells with their wives. The three Dooley brothers—James, Esom and George—hugged their father and

The Oxford train depot, circa 1859. From its platforms, hundreds of young men, resplendent in their brightly regaled uniforms, polished brass buttons and feathered Hardee hats, stepped onto the trains and into history. *Courtesy of Special Collections, University of Mississippi Libraries.*

anxious mother, promising victory and glory. There was Second Corporal James H. Howry, Privates Dudley Isom, Charles B. Neilsen and Thomas P. Buford, all of whom reassured their families and swore to come back to them. Then there were brothers Jim and Frank Dailey, whose folks came up from Holmes County for the sendoff, and Dailey's childhood friend, Jeremiah Gage, who bid his own farewells to his father, Matthew; mother, Patience; sister, Mary; five siblings; and his girlfriend. They boarded amid boundless cheering and tearful goodbyes.

As the train groaned forward, it moved with ever increasing speed down the track, the drivers pumping, the cars rumbling by, brakes squealing, steam hissing, sparks and black smoke rising, a steady rhythm moving onward, until finally the last car sped by as its wind pulled at the people's clothing as if to try and carry them along. The whistle shrieked and the band played; arms and hands and flags and ribbons waved and mixed together; and cheers erupted and huzzahs repeated over and over until it all congealed into one single, continuous cacophony of sound. In that moment, hanging tideless like a drop of the purest rain suspended perfectly in space and time, everyone who was there would forever remember it as the most glorious and unrivaled of moments, the high-water mark of their Southern pride as Oxford sent its young men off to war.

CHAPTER 4

THE FAR SUMMER THUNDER

*"As man cannot love and cherish woman bereft of honor, so woman cannot
reverence and honor man devoid of courage."*
—*Sallie Wiley, March 9, 1861*

L ong after the Lamar Rifles and the University Greys departed for the
front, Lafayette County continued to field additional units to the war.
They were always tearful farewells at the Oxford depot, with each departure
becoming more routine than the one before. Companies like the Magnolia
Guards, the McClung Riflemen, Thompson's Cavalry, the Paris Rebels,
the Pegues Defenders and the Dave Rogers Rifles received their orders and
shipped out for their different assignments. By fall, eleven companies in all
had passed through the depot and were actively engaged in the fighting. In
the end, more than twenty-two hundred young Lafayette County men—
most of whom were no more than twenty years old—had gone.

It was a time when the enemy was far away from Oxford, and the
thought of the war coming to Mississippi was inconceivable. The main
expectation most people had was that the war, in all its presumed
awfulness, would be over before the fall harvest. In this idealistic view, the
Southern armies would be victorious in the East; the Confederate States
of America would be recognized; and all the boys from the regiments
who had won the prize would come home to a heroic homecoming. It
was an expectation kept all the more alive by all the hopeful mothers and
daughters on the home front who convinced themselves that *their* sons,
husbands or beaus, were going to come home. Even as disturbing reports

of terrible battles emerged in the papers, no one allowed himself to think the unthinkable.

As the summer passed, quiet settled upon the town unlike any it had known before. The frantic mobilization had taken its toll on the male population. Merchants like Robert H. Wyatt, Silas Owens and Andrew Ragland no longer were there to sell goods to the men and ladies of the town. Clerks Henry Sheegog, Joseph Robertson and Gabriel Smither weren't there either. Some children were schooled at home now because their regular teachers— men like James Gilmore, Isaac Listenbee and James Kendall—had gone off to fight. Farmers like James Graham, John W. House and William Pierce no longer bought the supplies or provisions they usually did nor did they plow and work their fields. The *Oxford Intelligencer* stopped publishing its weekly paper at the end of May, as both of its editors, Howard Falconer and Frank Duval, had enlisted and were gone to the war. Lafayette County deputy sheriff David Moseley was gone, as was telegrapher Charles Gaston and even tombstone agent H.R. Mendenhall. By the autumn of 1861, the once-teeming county seat had become an empty town of women, children and old men.

In the wake of all the departures, a new kind of mobilization began to take hold of the residents. Older men formed units of the home guard and patrolled the town, and boys too young for military service created their own cadet corps in anticipation of someday getting into the fight. Robert Sheegog Jr., elected captain of the Avent Cadets, managed to recruit several dozen boys, drilling them in the square in their blue-trimmed, grey-flannel uniforms with red-striped, white trousers. Young Edmonia Carter presented their flag to them in a lavish evening ceremony. Oxford threw them a grand Cadet Ball, where they danced, laughed and enjoyed themselves, "forgetting the war cloud hovering over our sunny South." With grim optimism, one of the last issues of the *Intelligencer* praised the spirit of the young cadets: "We rejoice to see this military spirit manifested among the boys…Ere three years roll around they may be called upon to fill vacancies made by their fathers and brothers slain in battle."

The Seed Corn of the Republic

But while many in Oxford were caught up in the patriotism of the times, Chancellor Frederick Barnard stood at his office window in the observatory and stared out in disbelief upon his deserted campus. All the students were gone, vanished like a dream in the waking light of morning. He assumed the office of chancellor with the goal of turning the University of Mississippi into an institution that would be the envy of the world. By 1861, he was well on his way to achieving that goal. He had created a graduate school, a new law school and, above all, instituted a new major emphasis on science. This included vast new collections of rare geological specimens and one-of-a-kind scientific instruments. The observatory he now looked out of he designed himself after the Pulkovo Observatory in St. Petersburg, Russia, fitted it out with the largest telescope in the world: an eight-inch Newtonian by Troughton & Simms of London. Now his world was coming apart— classrooms were empty, dormitories deserted.

He had done his best to keep the students from leaving. After receiving letters from parents expressing their concerns that their underage sons had signed up for military service, Barnard used the occasion to write each enrolled student, reminding the underage ones of the illegality of their actions and pleading with the regular students to remain steadfast in their studies for the sake of the community. He realized very quickly that if the students went off to war, the university would have to close. The world he had known for so many years was disintegrating before his eyes, and he blamed it on the war and its "wretched victims of a folly without a parallel in history." In the weeks following secession, he had written to Governor Pettus, requesting that the University Greys *not* be activated for military service. Jefferson Davis, who by now was president of the Confederate States, had likewise received a letter from Barnard, complaining about the inane rationale of sending students to war. Davis agreed with him on every point. "Enrolling our young men in the military," he wrote back, "is like grinding the seed corn of the Republic."

With the president on his side, Barnard now turned to Pettus, expecting him to follow suit. He had a reason to be hopeful. William Lowry's repeated requests to the governor for officer commissions and activation to state service had been turned down numerous times since their formation in December 1860. When no word had come, Levins Bisland wrote his own letter to the governor pleading to be taken into service. "For God's sake," he wrote. "Let us go, and I give you my word that you shall never blush for shame of the University Greys." By late April, the governor had caved in, and he mobilized the Greys for active service. In the end, all the arrows that had been in Frederick Barnard's quiver could not possibly fell the beast that ultimately consumed his entire student body. The minutes of the university faculty meeting for May 2, 1861, read like an account of the last gasps of a dying man. Barnard reported that since the departure of the University Greys and Lamar Rifles, "nearly all the other students have taken out

The class of 1861 in front of the professor's residence and student dormitory, taken during the early months of secession. By summer, all of them were all gone. More than half would die in the killing that was to come. None of those who survived the war ever returned to their university studies. *Courtesy of Special Collections, University of Mississippi Libraries.*

'dismissions' or leaves of absence." Only five students remained, he said, "and they would probably drop off in a few hours." They did.

By June, the University of Mississippi was a ghost town. The faculty granted graduating students their degrees in bachelor of law and bachelor of arts, then broke for summer recess. When they convened again on September 18, 1861, only four students presented themselves for matriculation. It was the final straw. On October 1, 1861, the trustees unconditionally accepted the resignations of Barnard, Lamar, Boynton and most of the other faculty members. Barnard quickly headed North with passes from Governor Pettus and Jefferson Davis. Professor E.C. Boynton was not so lucky. Like Barnard, his sentiments were with the North. But he and his family were quickly put under house arrest, given only a few hours to pack and then were hustled to the state line. The Boyntons were forced to leave most of their possessions behind, including Professor Boynton's valuable photographic equipment and glass plates. The Southern professors meanwhile, faced with the prospect of war, could only contemplate their own fate.

The First Casualty

Lucius Lamar was thirty-six years old in 1861, and, for the first time in his life, he found himself suddenly unemployed and without anything to do. The war had come as he feared it would and with it came a psychological disruption that thrust him into a period of melancholia and inaction. After resigning from Congress in February, he came back to Oxford to a nonexistent law practice and plantation holdings that did not produce anything resembling measurable financial security. As a partial remedy, he presided over classes of constitutional law and moral philosophy at the University of Mississippi during the spring session. When not teaching, he retreated to his plantation Solitude near Abbeville on the banks of the Tallahatchie and tried to work. But even there, he found little to do that gave him the kind of intellectual stimulation and purpose in life he had always depended on. He never had much interest in plantation affairs anyway and considered them base and boring. He hadn't lived at Solitude since he went away to Congress in 1857, and though he had contemplated retiring altogether from politics to tend to his plantation—a move that would make him a rich man—he simply had no taste for it. Now sitting in his plantation office gazing out at the lethargic Tallahatchie as it slipped past his window, he began to feel that he, too, was somehow being passed by.

Then his law partner, Christopher H. Mott, a veteran of the Mississippi Rifles in the war with Mexico, suggested he join him in a venture to organize a new regiment of Mississippians for the war. The new regiment would be raised for service "during the war," meaning it would be a regiment of Mississippians raised for national service rather than under state authority. The idea must have appealed to Lamar because he soon volunteered as Mott's second in command. By the middle of May, recruitment had achieved sufficient numbers for the regiment to receive their commissions and be called up to service. It would consist of ten companies of about one hundred men each, totaling one thousand men in all. Mott's Guards, raised by Mott and Lucius Lamar from Lafayette County, became Company B and would be joined by two other Lafayette County companies: the McClung Riflemen and the Avent Southrons, designated as Companies E and F respectively. Also in the new regiment were the President Davis Guards (Company A), the Warren Rifles (Company C), Thomas Hinds Guards (Company D), Panola Invincibles (Company G), Salem Dragoons (Company H), Marshall Rifles (Company I) and the Jake Thompson Guards (Company K). These were brought together to become the Nineteenth Mississippi Infantry Regiment.

Up until this time, Lamar had allowed his young son—also named Lucius—to drill along with his father and the Mott's Guards on the campus of the University of Mississippi. Lamar, who was a caring and devoted father, indulged his young son, perhaps excessively. He had the boy fitted with his own small uniform, complete with small hat and sword and a wooden pistol and included him as "one of the boys." On May 25, 1861, when the order came from Montgomery, the Confederate capital, that the company was being called into service, his father broke the news to young Lucius that he was too young to go to war and would have to stay behind. Former slave Jane Wilburn, who often sat on the fence and watched the company drill, remembered "My sakes, he hollered and yelled sumthin' terrible. It lak to er kilt him when dey tel' him he couldn't go too." The boy took it hard. As the company loaded onto the train at the depot, the elder Lamar leaned out the window and waved to his wife Virginia and young son. The boy, resigned to being left behind, yelled out to his father, "Be sure to catch old Lincoln an' bring me his head!"

The Nineteenth Mississippi had been only the latest of many military organizations from Lafayette County to pass through the Oxford depot. It made a quick stop in Montgomery and then proceeded to Richmond, arriving on June 1. There, the regiment encamped at the fairgrounds outside the city, where the whole landscape teemed with populations of young soldiers in grey. Lieutenant Colonel Lamar seems to have spent little time with the regiment, however, preferring instead to ride into the city to visit friends. In the Spotswood Hotel, President Davis welcomed him, and the two spent hours in friendly banter, reminiscing of old times and engaging in political discussion. These visits were intellectual balm for the fire-eater from Georgia, who hadn't had that kind of mental stimulation since he was in Congress, and he once more realized what it was that made him happy and gave him the high purpose he sought. "Grand, glorious old commonwealth!" he bellowed one evening from Davis's open window to a crowd that had come to serenade the Confederate president. "Mother of States…standing here in robes of steel, raising a majestic arm to press back the foe that dare attempt to force her daughters into an unnatural and unwilling union!" It was the old Lamar at his rhetorical best, cloaked in the righteousness of the cause and fully believing in it as did the cheering, applauding crowd below.

His visits into Richmond were frequent from then on. The forays also included long, lingering evenings and weekends spent with an old friend, former U.S. congressman James Chestnut and his wife, Mary. Mary Chestnut described a Lamar who arrived late in the evening insisting he could only stay a few minutes before having to return to his regiment, but whose visits often lingered well into the night. She recalled in her diary that he came at eight o'clock in the evening "but at twelve he was still talking to us on the sofa." She also recorded a Lucius Lamar his friends rarely saw, one who seemed, from time to time, to have even had his doubts about slavery and the course the South was on. On those occasions, he would slip into a melancholy mood and lament that while he believed in the inherent rights of the South to maintain slavery, the institution had become "too heavy a load for us to carry." He never doubted what he often considered as the "soundness of the system." Yet deep down, he had known for some time now that their "peculiar institution" was living on borrowed time, and he was convinced it would never survive a war.

He rode back to his camp that night under the light of a full moon to rejoin Mott and the regiment, its tents darkened and campfires little more than glowing embers. He knew the visits into the city had to end at some point and he would ultimately have to go to the front. He had no fear of it. Honor dictated he not let himself fear it nor even consider backing down from the responsibilities inherent in his position. Nearly a thousand men depended on him. Yet, while he gave it his complete devotion, army life—to say the least—did not agree with Lucius Lamar. It put him out of his element and isolated him from the intellectual circles he depended on for mental stimulation. The ordinariness of it bored him and he found its perfunctory nature frustrating. He wasn't able to comprehend, for instance, military tactics and strategy, and the myriads of regulations just puzzled him. Each morning he arose and commenced upon the stultifying duties that necessarily went with keeping hundreds of bored young men busy and out of mischief. His enlistment was for one year, and Lamar, like the many back in Oxford, hoped the war would be over before then.

On the evening of July 1, 1861, Lamar was in his tent about to retire, when he felt a sudden rush to his head followed by dizziness, disorientation and massive headache. Alarmed, he called for an aide to come, and as he did so, a violent vertigo seized him and threw him to the ground. A lieutenant found him unconscious and helped him up onto his cot. When he awoke, he found he was paralyzed on one side, and when he tried to speak, his words were slurred and unintelligible. The camp surgeon was summoned and, after some examination, it was determined he had suffered an attack of what was called "apoplexy." He had suffered a similar attack back in 1859 and had even traveled to Paris to seek treatment for what was later described as "cerebral disease." Lacking complete medical data on the case, the symptoms seem to indicate he suffered a stroke, but whether it was a congenital defect or the result of the stress and physical hardship of soldiering, the condition would plague him for the rest of his life. On July 9, as he was recovering, his regiment struck tents and moved out toward the front where Union and Confederate troops were amassing, leaving him behind. Realizing it was to be a long recovery for his friend, Colonel Mott determined the best treatment would be to send him back to Oxford until he was able to rejoin the regiment. A few days later, Lamar left Richmond for home, not knowing what was to become of him.

IMPERISHABLE GLORY

Not far from where the Nineteenth Mississippi was encamped, the University Greys and Lamar Rifles had likewise arrived at the front and were moving up closer to the fighting. Only ten weeks earlier they had set out from Oxford with the memory of that glorious day still fresh and clear in their minds. The train had taken them to Corinth, where they were incorporated into the Eleventh Regiment, Mississippi Volunteer Infantry. The University Greys became Company A and the Lamar Rifles, Company G. From Corinth, they traveled by train across the country, ending up at Harpers Ferry, the scene of the famous John Brown Raid. They were then thrown together with thousands of other young men from all over the South—boys from Alabama, Tennessee and Virginia—and they saw more military uniforms of different varieties than they ever imagined. Finally, they were absorbed into General B.E. Bee's Third Brigade under General Joseph E. Johnston's Army of the Shenandoah. With them in Bee's Brigade were the Second Mississippi, Fourth Alabama and First Tennessee Regiments.

In their first weeks in Virginia, soldier life for many Lafayette County companies seemed easy and light. "I am perfectly green as to my duty," wrote one bewildered soldier to his uncle. W.E. Duncan wrote that General Johnston had been watching the Eleventh Mississippi and declared them "one of the best looking regiments he had ever seen." Another note written July 13, 1861, from Captain John M. Lyles of the Magnolia Guards to his wife asked her to come to Virginia to visit him. "You may think, or some folks may say," he explained, "that our soldiers have a hard time of it, but it is a mistake; save sickness and guard duties, we do nearly as well as if at home."

But the honeymoon was short-lived. On July 18, 1861, General Johnston, still six miles to the west at Winchester, received word that Federal troops under General Irvin McDowell had crossed the Potomac and were advancing against General P.T. Beauregard near a place called Manassas Junction, about twenty-five miles southwest of Washington. Johnston knew that the quickest conclusion to the war was for the Federals to capture Richmond; his objective was now first to prevent any further movement by McDowell into Virginia and, second, to destroy his army if possible. Mobilizing his division of nearly twelve thousand men, he dispatched them to Beauregard's aid with all speed. "We are making all efforts to reinforce you," read the dispatch, informing Beauregard that "Hampton's Legion, McRae's Regiment, and two battalions—Mississippi and Alabama" were on their way. Beauregard, with just twenty thousand men, faced McDowell's thirty-five thousand Federal troops across Bull Run Creek. With the addition of Johnston's twelve thousand fresh troops, the armies would be nearly equal in strength.

Johnston arrived at Manassas around noon on July 20, accompanied by General Bee's Brigade, consisting of the Fourth and Second Alabama and two companies from the Eleventh Mississippi: the Noxubee Rifles and the University Greys. By the time they arrived, the fighting for the day was concluding and both sides were falling back for the night. It was clear to many that a major engagement was underway, which just might determine the future of the Confederacy. Captain William Lowry and his men pitched camp that night in the fields below Bull Run Creek. Amid the sounds of hammering tent spikes, horses and unhitching supply wagons, one soldier later wrote they could still hear in the distance "the last volleys of musketry dying away." Many were disappointed to have missed the fight, but they knew the morning would present the chance they sought to prove themselves. That night, as the moon rose over the misty woods east of Bull Run Creek, the men of the University Greys were but one small company among hundreds that made up the Confederate force of nearly thirty thousand strong.

Within each camp, the young soldiers did what young soldiers do before a fight: write letters, think of home, dream about girls, play cards, gamble and sing songs. Companies that hadn't seen battle yet were more likely to sing patriotic songs to keep their spirits high. Love songs were always in demand, and one that had special appeal on both sides was the beautiful, yearning melody *Aura Lea*. Men like Captain William Lowry, Lieutenant Levins Bisland, First Sergeant Henry M. Rice and Private Mitchell A. Reynolds all sang it, thinking of being home in Oxford. No doubt a few of the others thought of the farewell note they had once penned to young Eliza Pegues before they left Oxford. "Goodbye," it said. "May peace around you spread her wings." Before long, the fires were out and the men had drifted off to sleep. The forced march they had endured that day made sure they slept soundly. One soldier who later wrote home said simply, "we were so tired we could have slept anywhere."

By nine o'clock the next morning, the Federal army was on the move again. Beauregard's plan, which he had devised the night before, had become useless. That was because McDowell had unexpectedly split his forces, sending Brigadier General Tyler's division directly down Warrenton Pike to threaten the Confederate center, while two other divisions commanded by Colonels Porter and Heintzelman deployed far out to the west and swung southward in a giant arc to assault the Confederate left flank. It had been under cover of Tyler's diversionary movement that Porter and Heintzelman's flanking divisions managed to cross Bull Run at Sudley Springs Ford almost undetected. Once Johnston realized the maneuver, he ordered his main forces to engage the Federal advance on his flank at once, while smaller forces and the natural barrier of Bull Run Creek held off Tyler's smaller diversionary attack. The first brigade to engage the Federals was Colonel Evans on Matthews Hill. Despite his eleven companies and two fieldpieces, he encountered stiff resistance and was pressed hard by an overwhelming force of Federal infantry and cannon. Johnston, knowing he must consolidate his line if he ever hoped to defeat the main Federal force, ordered General Bee and Colonel Bartow to link up with Evans.

Things then began to happen where the Mississippi troops waited. Orders echoed through the air and companies sprang to their feet, shouldered their rifles and began to move. The Mississippi boys, still waiting in the Confederate rear, knew it would not be long now; they would finally get the chance for glory they had been seeking since they left Oxford. They were anxious, excited and scared, but ready to go. None of them knew what to expect. War, for them, was still like an exciting, attractive maiden waiting to be courted. But in that small, fixed moment before they advanced and the killing began, as they waited, hunched down, clutching their rifles in the tense, smoke-filled shade beneath the trees, waiting for the word to go—as the sound of cannon and musket fire grew louder and the smell of powder and sweat permeated the air—the only world they had ever known suddenly rushed back upon them. It was a world they once knew and wished they didn't have to let go of, yet they knew at last they must. In it they still heard the voices of their mothers and remembered the sunlit memories of home; they heard bands playing and saw the crowds cheering and the young ladies of Oxford waving at them as they marched past them in their grey-clad glory.

The Far Summer Thunder

There were the goodbyes and the promises and the assurances of coming back when it was all over. They had become the gods of the moment, the elite of their country, the salvation of the South. Then, as suddenly as it had come, the moment rushed away from them again and was gone. In its place were the growing sounds of distant battle, and it left all the young men staring at each other with a sudden, profound dread.

General Bee abruptly halted his horse nearby and shouted orders to a group of officers. The Greys found themselves suddenly up on their feet and with the rest of the brigade they advanced west along a line parallel to Bull Run Creek. Then at the double-quick, Captain Lowry and his lieutenants led them onward until they at last reached Warrenton Turnpike where Bee quickly formed them up, placing their left against a stone house and dressing their ranks to the right until they formed a continuous line with Colonel Francis S. Bartow's Georgians on their right. Then, in one movement like a great undulating wave, their battle line moved across the open field and up Matthews Hill, where they formed on Evans's Brigade and became a mile-long barrier of grey steel. But as their front ranks came over the rise, they ran into a sudden wall of blue. Privates Jim Dailey, Parmeno Harding and Junius S. Meek felt the minie balls nicking and tearing at their uniforms as they tried to advance. Out in front through the thick smoke were Lieutenants McCaleb, Raines and Bisland, swords hiked high over their heads, trying to keep everyone in a straight line, bellowing out orders to load and "fire on command" as they were trained. Suddenly, there was a new experience: the peculiar "whirring" sound that Federal minie balls made as they passed just inches past their heads. Then, to the right and to the left, boys began falling to the ground.

It soon became evident to every soldier on that hill that they were up against an overwhelming force. On the Confederate left, Evans faced the First and Second Brigades of Colonels Porter and Franklin; General Bee slugged away at Colonel Ambrose Burnside's Second Brigade in the center; and Colonel Bartow fought off Colonel Willcox on the right. The Confederate line employed thirteen regiments plus three batteries overall, yet the Federal line opposing them, which contained an estimated eighteen thousand men, continued to grow in apparent strength, reinforced by what seemed to be a limitless reserve of fresh troops. To make matters worse, the Federal Third Brigade under Colonel William T. Sherman had managed to cross Bull Run Creek behind them and slam into the right flank of Bartow's Brigade, killing hundreds and sending the rest of the Confederate line into mass confusion. Some of the Greys watched, dreamlike, as Private Junius Meek fell lifeless into the tall grass, then Privates George M. Moseley and Richard C. Bridges fell. Others in the Greys, like Sergeant Henry M. Rice and Private Richard C. Bridges, were struck and dropped to the ground. Private Calvin Myers fell wounded, as did Private Mitchell Reynolds. Lieutenant Levins Bisland, whom everyone liked for his passionate patriotism, was struck fatally as he shouted orders for the ranks to reload, falling backward into the grass in a distorted, rumpled heap.

On down the line, grey uniforms fell one by one. As the bloodbath continued, the Confederate line was eventually pressed so hard that it began to fall back upon itself like a paper ribbon that folds up in the wind. Realizing all at once they had no other clear choice but to withdraw and try to regroup, the masses of grey men pulled back through the smoke and haze of the hill, still firing, until they reached a reinforced position atop Henry House Hill. There, General Bee encountered Colonel Thomas J. Jackson, standing calmly among his field artillery and brigade of Virginians. "The enemy is driving us," Bee exclaimed excitedly. Jackson, standing perfectly calm as the musketry, shot and shell exploded around him, replied matter-of-factly, "Then sir, we shall give them the bayonet." Bee admired Jackson's apparent lack of fear and turned to his own men, perhaps to inspire them, and pointing to Jackson's Virginians shouted, "Look at Jackson's men, standing like a stone wall!" As Bee turned to rejoin his men, he, too, was struck down by a Federal minie ball.

For a brief time, the presence of Jackson and a sudden appearance on the field of General Johnston helped to give the men a renewed confidence in the deadly work they were engaged in. But Federal canister, shot and shell continued to rain down upon them from the particularly deadly Griffin and Ricketts Batteries opposite their position on Matthews Hill. It became some matter of pressing concern to Johnston and his division commanders to silence the two batteries. Griffin's guns lay directly across the field from where the Greys had reformed and were now pressing against the Federal line. At one point in the action, the University Greys charged Griffin's Battery, capturing the cannon as much with their rebel yell as at the point of the bayonet. A Virginia company charged Ricketts Battery nearby, which also was captured. And as the battle continued to rage, control of these two key gun positions would change hands many times. But by mid-afternoon, the Confederates held them for good, and McDowell's troops were put into flight. "I had full confidence in the skill and indomitable courage of General Beauregard," Johnston wrote in his offical report, "...the high soldierly qualities of Gens. Bee and Jackson and Col. Evans, and the devoted patriotism of their troops."

The Far Summer Thunder

It rained for days after the battle. Confederate losses at Manassas were 387 killed, 1,582 wounded and 13 captured or missing. General Bee, who had been shot on Henry House Hill, was taken to his headquarters after the battle and died the following morning. Of the University Greys, 5 had been killed and at least 4 wounded. Lieutenant Levins Bisland—the one who had written to Governor Pettus before the war and said, "For God's sake let us go!"—died in a field hospital, as did Private Sterling Tarpley; the rest died where they fell on the field. A few of those wounded were eventually captured and became prisoners of war.

The Greys and the Rifles sought the war, and the war finally touched them as war does to soldiers who get too close. It brought death among their ranks. It also brought them the glory they sought. Afterward, the exploits of the Greys appeared in newspapers all across the South. The University of Mississippi Trustees could not help but recognize the price so dearly paid by so many of their former students. In the newspaper they had printed the notice: "The University Greys, late of the University of Mississippi, have covered themselves in imperishable glory."

CHAPTER 5

THE BELEAGUERED CITY

"If God is against us, we are ruined forever."
—*Albert H. Clark, Forty-second Mississippi, April 27, 1862*

After Manassas, it was clear to everyone the war was not going to be a short one. Yet, there still existed the perception among some in Lafayette County—especially among young men still wanting to fight—that it might end before the opportunity presented itself to enlist. Even after the brutal events at Manassas, and as battle after battle thereafter appeared in the newspapers, enlistments continued to rise all across the South. James F. Dooley was one who, along with friends, rushed off to join the Lamar Rifles. Willis Lea, John H. Ivy and William F. Smith similarly joined the University Greys, along with fifteen other men from Oxford. By early 1862, the Confederate government, realizing it was going to be a long, protracted conflict, made a strong appeal to those with twelve-month enlistments—like Jeremiah Gage and Jim Dailey of the University Greys—to reenlist "for the war." As an incentive, the government offered furloughs and bonuses, but most signed on the line regardless of incentives. At the same time, the Confederate government passed the first conscription law, calling into service every man aged eighteen to thirty-five. To Rebecca Pegues, it meant that all of her cousins and young nephews would have to go and fight. But like everyone else in Lafayette County, she, too, began to realize that the war was exacting a heavy toll, noting in her diary, "We now have to use every effort against our merciless enemy."

In early 1862, the war in all its awfulness finally came to Oxford. It had been coming gradually, like a storm that first appears indistinctly on the horizon, then grows in darkness and intensity as it nears until all at once it is upon you and consumes you in its violence. Its coming began as Federal forces pushed southward from St. Louis, Missouri, down the Tennessee River, capturing Forts Henry and Donelson along the way. The advancing Union forces compelled Confederate general Albert Sidney Johnston to pull out of western Kentucky and Tennessee and concentrate his own army of nearly forty-four thousand at Corinth, establishing a new defensive line east to west along the Memphis and Charleston Railroad, the only remaining link to the capital in Richmond. As a Federal force of forty thousand led by Major General Ulysses S. Grant moved down the Tennessee, Johnston deployed his forces from Corinth northward to engage the Federals and hopefully drive them back. With Johnston was General P.T. Beauregard, the hero of Manassas, and an aid-de-camp named Colonel Jacob Thompson. Thompson, like Lucius Lamar, had offered his services to the Confederate army and found himself traveling north with Beauregard through the tranquil Tennessee countryside to meet the northern army. Johnston finally found Grant at Pittsburgh Landing with his back against the river. A well-coordinated attack on such terrain might serve to drive him into the river and destroy the Union army.

The attack came on Sunday, April 6, 1862, centering in the area around the small church called Shiloh. It was a bloody affair, each side hammering away at the other, with Johnston gaining ground early because of superior artillery support. While leading an attack against the Federal left, Johnston suddenly wheeled in his saddle and fell from his horse, struck by a stray bullet. The commander of Confederate forces bled to death a short time later. Command of the Army of Mississippi now fell to Beauregard. By the end of the first day, was badly beaten up. As night came and rain poured onto the battlefield, he consolidated his forces in a new, well-defended line near the river at Pittsburgh Landing.

That same evening, a confident Beauregard telegraphed President Davis announcing "a complete victory." He had the enemy right where he wanted him, he said, and planned to finish him off in the morning. What Beauregard did not know was that as he was sending his telegraph message, Grant received critical reinforcements during the night from General Buell's army, whom he had been trying to link up with. This brought the Federal fighting strength up to 55,000 men, a third of them fresh troops. The next morning, unaware of the Federal reinforcement, Beauregard launched his attack against Grant with only 28,000 men. The second day of the battle was a bloodbath for the Confederates. Much has been speculated about Beauregard's "lost opportunities" at Shiloh, such as his failure to survey the front lines, calling off the previous day's battle early and his lack of a cohesive battle plan for the second day of fighting. In the end, as Confederate forces retreated back to Corinth, 1,728 Confederate soldiers were dead, 8,012 wounded and 959 captured or missing.

The Injured and the Dead

When the news reached the people of Oxford that there had been a great battle at Shiloh, Tennessee, the first reaction was shock. That such a large enemy force had penetrated so deeply into the South so as to now threaten Mississippi itself seemed incomprehensible. Although it initially caused some panic, at the same time it also became the engine that propelled everyone to begin taking greater steps in supporting the war effort. Corinth soon swelled with the wounded, and those that could not be cared for were sent down the line to Oxford. The notification that casualties were coming resulted in no small amount of rushing and hurrying about the town to prepare for their arrival. As if by coordinated effort, women stripped beds in their own homes of mattresses, bedsheets, quilts, pillows and anything that might be of value to the care of the sick and wounded; young girls scraped lint for bandages; and older men came forward to pick up these items and drive them by wagon to where they were needed. It was determined that the vacant and unused buildings of the University of Mississippi were ideal facilities for a hospital, and it became everyone's rushed focus to make the preparations. With Chancellor Barnard and most of the faculty gone, the trustees had appointed Dr. Quinche as the custodian of campus facilities, assisted by Dr. Eugene W. Hilgard, late the state geologist of Mississippi and now appointed by Governor Pettus to be guardian of the state collections and the valuable scientific apparatus. They immediately went to work.

The chapel would be the first building to be outfitted for hospital use. Mattresses, bed frames and supplies donated by the men and women of the town were brought in and hauled up the stairs and set up in the empty rooms. Lucius Lamar petitioned Governor Pettus to appoint Dr. Thomas Isom as chief surgeon and Dr. Henry Branham as his assistant. Soon after, a staff of doctors was assembled consisting of Dr. Gillespie from Granada, and Drs. Chandler, Phipps, Stover, Brown, King and Buffington of Oxford. Immediately, Isom and Branham began determining how the arriving wounded would be processed, treated and assigned. The Lyceum, that once proud centerpiece of the University with its stately, white columned facade,

The Chapel, Oxford's first war hospital. Here Dr. Thomas Isom tried to save many of the young Confederate boys who were wounded at the bloodbath that was Shiloh. An almost daily procession carried the dead to burial in the Confederate cemetery on the south side of campus. *Courtesy of Special Collections, University of Mississippi Libraries.*

was converted into a dispensary where the sick were treated and surgeries were performed. Medicines and tinctures were supplied from the drugstore on the square owned by Dr. King's father.

Assistants were also needed, and Isom began training ordinary women from the town who volunteered to serve as nurses. They received minimal training, then were assigned wards and took turns tending the sick and bringing them soup, food, water, milk and even cake and confectionaries. Each ward also had one Negro and a convalescent soldier who helped in whatever capacity was necessary. The house directly behind the Lyceum, which was the residence of the professor of chemistry and kept by a Mrs. Davidson, became the mess hall where Isom and his surgeons, assistants and nurses gathered to grab a late cup of coffee or to eat after the long, exhaustive days that seemed never to end. From time to time, little May Davidson would circulate among the tables of surgeons with a basket of

The University of Mississippi Lyceum, 1860. Originally housing all the classrooms and faculty offices before the Civil War, it was converted into a dispensary for wounded after the Battle of Corinth in 1862. It was subsequently used as a hospital by Union forces under General Ulysses S. Grant and later by General Nathan Bedford Forrest's cavalry. *Courtesy of Special Collections, University of Mississippi Libraries.*

warm biscuits, saying, "Have a biscuit? Don't take two!" Many of them slept at the dispensary or anywhere on campus where they could find a bed to be near in case of necessity. Others, like Isom and King, went home at night, their horses remembering the way and bringing them safely to their doorstep even after they fell asleep from exhaustion.

Committees of citizens met at the campus and were assigned to meet the daily trains. The wounded that came into Oxford arrived at the same depot that, only a year before, had been the scene of glorious departures of Lafayette County's military companies. Now, hundreds of grim-faced soldiers, far away from their own homes, passed over the same hallowed ground where once had trodden Oxford's patriots. Instead of bright-colored uniforms and confident faces, there were fearful expressions, bandaged heads and hands and legs, rumpled uniforms, torn, ripped away or, in some cases, missing altogether. All were darkened by the soil and grime of battle. By May 1862, the entire town began aching with wounded as trainload after trainload arrived from Corinth.

Dr. Isom and his team developed an efficient process to handle the incoming sick and wounded. It began at the trains, where patients were unloaded and placed on wagons and driven to campus. There they were examined and treated in the dispensary, categorized by the nature of their wounds or illness and finally assigned to a building and a bed. But it became clear that as casualties flooded in, more room was needed. Every building on campus eventually was converted in some way to accommodate the growing numbers. This included three additional dormitories that once were home to dozens of students like Private Junius Meek, Private Mitchell Reynolds and Sergeant Jeremiah Gage. Now they were filled to capacity with wounded and the dying. The professor's residence, where Chancellor Barnard and his wife once lived and entertained, was likewise transformed. Eventually the observatory, too, was filled to capacity. As summer turned to autumn, there seemed to be no end to the steady stream of war-wounded men who flooded into Oxford.

Of the more than fifteen hundred Confederate casualties that came through the university hospital, almost half of them would not survive. Once the scene of high-spirited youth, scholarly attainment and Southern gallantry, the campus soon became a graveyard filled with the dead. The Magnetic Observatory, situated next to the observatory building, became the last stop for the dead and subsequently became known as the Dead House. In the beginning, corpses were treated with respect—socks pinned at the toes, hands folded across the breast, eyes closed and jaw tied up—then they were loaded onto a litter and carted off to the Dead House. There, William Jenkins handled the details of burial, verifying and reporting the identity of each soldier before mating them to a coffin. Then Jenkins loaded it onto a flat wagon and transported the remains across campus to a burial ground that had been marked off on the south side of campus. Negroes dug the graves and assisted Jenkins and his helpers lower the box into the ground with ropes and then properly mark the grave with the name of the deceased. Jenkins eventually left his job, and these duties fell to someone else. Eventually, a rude pine box hammered together by Negroes replaced the coffins, and later even that became a luxury. As the number of hospital dead grew, corpses were simply thrown onto a wagon, carted away and, as one slave who was there remembered, "they just buried them in bunches like dead chickens." Amputated limbs were carted away from the Lyceum in wheelbarrows and dumped in a hole nearby to be covered over and forgotten.

By early summer, the war, it seemed, not only was approaching from the north, but also from the south, as news of the capture of New Orleans and

Natchez jolted an already uneasy population. The captures cut off vital supply lines and communication routes that the Confederate river states depended on. Many of the medicines and other supplies Dr. Isom and his hospital team relied upon for treatment of the wounded now began to run out and were not replaced. King's drugstore on the square was unable to get any more quinine, morphine, ether, chloroform or other essentials from their supplier in Memphis, who, in turn, had obtained them from New Orleans. Other supply sources were just as hopeless. Even the Confederate government soon ran out of its stores, unable to procure any more except from ships running the blockade—and those did not make it to the inland towns either but were sent instead to the front lines.

To make do, the doctors and druggists manufactured what they needed from native herbs, roots, barks and leaves of plants collected from the area. The other alternative was to attempt to purchase from Southern ports those goods smuggled in by blockade runners that were not a priority to the Confederate government. But the hefty prices demanded for smuggled goods often made such purchases impossible. Inland towns, like Oxford, suffered most from lack of supplies. Whiskey and homemade wines seemed to be the one commodity that was somehow always on hand. Locals distilled corn to produce moonshine in abundant quantities, suitable for use as an anesthetic or painkiller. In the sewing group, Rebecca Pegues and other ladies made dyes from the indigo bush, berries and lichen. Mrs. King, wife of Dr. King, loomed her own cotton cloth and colored it with dye she made from a local tree bark. When Oxford was later occupied, one Union soldier was so impressed with the cloth, he offered her fifty dollars in gold for it. She refused, preferring—as she put it—to keep the cloth for "our boys."

The gradual depletion of all these resources was but the dark harbinger of things to come. The North was slowly strangling the South. By late April 1862, the Union army had entered Mississippi itself and taken Corinth, sending ever increasing numbers of sick and wounded to Oxford. An appeal went out from Dr. Isom to residents, asking more families to take in convalescing soldiers. "My father opened his country home to them," Ella Pegues remembered years later. "And when they recovered and returned to their commands or were sent home on furlough, he took others in their places." While the assigning of soldiers to homes opened up some bed space at the hospital, it was never enough. So many wounded arrived with the daily trains that Dr. Isom and his staff reached a point where they simply had no place to put them all. Governor Pettus, who happened to visit in May, was dumbfounded at the volume of wounded that had poured into the town. "The scene presented here is truly heart rending," he lamented. "No room. Crowded 730 sick in the Hospital, 230 sick and wounded left here last night on the cars—against my strongest remonstrance." The governor was, for once, powerless to do anything about it.

THE JUGGERNAUT

As 1862 wore on, the promises of victory in the field faded, and in its place came misfortune. The Union army had decimated the Confederates at Shiloh, captured Forts Donelson and Henry, and in late May, captured New Orleans without a fight. Corinth fell after a month-long siege, as did Tupelo, Iuka, Okolona and Memphis in June. Controlling northern Mississippi became part of a larger Union strategy designed to open up a logistical and communication highway for the North and at the same time split the Confederacy in two. Vicksburg became the last piece in the puzzle. It's strategic position overlooking a tight hairpin bend of the Mississippi gave it unique importance: Confederate batteries overlooking the river denied river traffic from going up or down. In order to win the war in the west, the Union had to take the city. "Vicksburg is the key," Lincoln had said. "The war can never be brought to a close until the key is in our pocket." Jefferson Davis likewise understood the necessity of holding the small Southern city on the bluff. "Vicksburg," he said, "is the nail head that holds the South's two halves together."

By autumn, the Union plan to move on Vicksburg went into motion. The Army of the Tennessee under the command of Major General Ulysses S. Grant began its march on November 2, 1862, snaking southward from Grand Junction, Tennessee, using the Mississippi Central Railroad for his supply line. The towns and cities that lay along that railroad suddenly found themselves in the path of a juggernaut, its mighty arms sweeping down, leviathan-like, consuming everything in its path. Grant's army was made up of nearly forty thousand effectives and was divided into a right wing under Major General William Tecumseh Sherman, a left wing under Brigadier General Charles S. Hamilton and a center wing under Major General James B. McPherson.

Oxford, Mississippi, lay directly in its path.

The Beleaguered City

REFUGEES AND CHATTELS

Throughout November, as Grant lumbered south, Lafayette County residents were completely mystified that their own army had done so little to defend them. Just south of the Tallahatchie near Abbeville, Confederate general John C. Pemberton's well-fortified line of defense was suddenly abandoned, pulling back toward Grenada. As the Southern army withdrew, women of the towns and in the countryside wept, some admonishing the retreating soldiers with reproofs and recriminations as the "most cowardly cavalry in the Confederacy." The troops had no choice but to keep going. Pemberton's march to Grenada left the whole of northern Mississippi exposed to the enemy, and it left Oxford and Lafayette County open to occupation and exploitation. Small units of local Confederate cavalry still patrolled in the area but they were completely ineffective as a defensive force.

Pemberton's retreat created a sudden fear and panic among the general population. In Oxford, an exodus of old men, women and children streamed out of town, following Pemberton's downcast sea of grey as it withdrew south down the muddy, rain-laden county roads toward Coffeyville, Grenada and beyond. Along the way, the Confederates left a path of destruction in their wake: cut telegraph lines, burned cotton, destroyed railroad trestles and burned bridges. Politicians and prominent figures of the county whose politics put them in danger of arrest by Northern forces simply fled. Jacob Thompson, Alexander Pegues and James Brown were forced to flee, leaving their wives and families to cope with the invading Yankees. Judge James Howry hitched his prized horses to his coach and sped out of town. Dr. Thomas Isom, after evacuating the last of the Confederate wounded from the university hospital, also left, leaving his wife, Sarah, to the mercy of the Yankees. Landowners packed up wagonloads of belongings, collected their slaves and abandoned their plantations. One Confederate officer witnessed the sorry masses "making their way south with their goods and chattels." The roads became jammed with refugees escaping for fear of their lives.

And so they left their beloved Oxford, streaming down the same roads that Peyton Jones and the early town commissioners had marked out in 1837; roads down which Jacob Thompson's record harvest of 392 bales of cotton were taken to market in 1859; roads that brought Lucius Lamar to Oxford in 1849 and which later carried him to Congress. They were roads that brought Augustus B. Longstreet and Frederick Barnard to the University of Mississippi, over which Dr. Isom drove his buggy on his rounds to visit patients like Eliza Pegues, who was often sick in bed. They were roads that had seen great things and roads that had seen terrible things, roads that Polly Cancer, Jane Wilburn, Joanna Thompson Isom and Lucindy Hall Shaw knew well and traveled frequently in their lives as slaves. Now those same roads—once the busy arteries of a thriving community—were reduced to little more than muddy lanes over which the frightened escaped, searching for a place where they could no longer feel afraid. These once proud, patriotic citizens of Oxford became refugees in their own homeland, reduced to formless figures like featureless shadows cast upon the ground, changed forever.

On November 8, word came that the Yankees had entered Mississippi at Hudsonville and were coming on fast. "Gloom hangs over us," wrote a lonely, frightened Rebecca Pegues from her plantation home near College Hill. "I just realized how nearly we are upon the evening of invasion. The enemy are at Holly Springs, and are expected to advance upon us with a large force." Another observer was convinced that the Confederate army "appears to have taken a stand, south of the Tallahatchie near Abbeville." But Rebecca Pegues was more realistic in her assessment. "We have an army it is true at the river—but they can scarcely hold their position."

By November 29, Grant was in Holly Springs. The leading edge of his forces extended six miles below the town to only a few miles above the Tallahatchie River. As Union cavalry advanced, they repaired the bridges, railroad tracks and trestles that had been damaged by the retreating Pemberton.

Both Sherman and Grant were somewhat surprised that resistance had been so light. On December 1, Grant telegraphed his General in Chief Halleck from Waterford: "Our cavalry are now crossing Tallahatchie. Infantry will follow immediately. The rebels are evidently retreating. If so, I will follow to Oxford. Our troops will be in Abbeville tomorrow, or a battle will be fought. Sherman is up and will cross the Tallahatchie at Wyatt." Grant still had suspicions that Pemberton might not, in fact, have withdrawn completely from his defensive position south of Holly Springs. The last thing he wanted to do was march his army into a trap, yet cavalry reconnaissance strongly indicated Pemberton was gone.

But as the Seventh Kansas—one of McPherson's lead cavalry brigades—came to the Tallahatchie, they bumped into a line of Confederate resistance behind earthworks designed to protect the Tallahatchie bridge. As a fight ensued, the Seventh's commander, Colonel Thomas P. Herrick, assuming he had run into Pemberton's forward line or perhaps his rear guard, called for reinforcements. "The rebel works are very strong at that point," he wrote in his report. But despite the exchange and the strong geographic position the earthworks commanded, Herrick quickly came to realize that the force within was merely a skirmish line. Rather than wait for the reinforcements, he ordered a flank movement by his right wing, which "compelled an evacuation without a battle." The Confederate defenders fled into the woods and disappeared. The Union army crossed the Tallahatchie and entered Lafayette County on December 1, 1862.

Meanwhile, Jacob Thompson, who had returned to Oxford briefly from service with the army, galloped through the county to the homes of landowners and the wealthy he knew, advising them to bring their silver and valuables to his house in Oxford at once. Having heard of atrocities and stories of looting and plundering by the Yankees, Thompson was determined to fight back, using a clever ruse to fool the Yankees. Years later, his seven-year-old house servant Joanna remembered how "Mr. Cullin an' Miss Pinkie Turner's father (William Turner), an' all de white folks put dey silver in boxes an' put dey names on hit." Thompson then had the boxes of silver stashed in the back room of his two-room office at his home. In the front room, he put one of the old slave grandmothers and a number of small, weeping slave children. On the front door, he posted a sign that read, "Small Pox in Here." Satisfied with the details, he mounted his horse and rode through the square up North Street to William Turner's house to observe the Union army as it approached.

Augustus B. Longstreet had been staying with his daughter and grandchildren at Solitude, Lamar's plantation on the Tallahatchie near Abbeville, when he learned about the approach of Grant's army. "My dear Lucius," he wrote his son-in-law in Virginia. "We are in a peck of troubles... Your plantation will soon be a battlefield. We shall be whipped on it, and the Yankees will make a desert of it." The pessimism in Longstreet's letter betrayed the feeling throughout most in Lafayette County, who by now had consigned themselves and their town to an inevitable fate that only eighteen months earlier seemed impossible. "It matters little," Longstreet concluded in his letter. "The prospect before us is awful." Packing his daughter, Virginia, and her children in a carriage, they left Lamar's plantation and fled to Columbus, Georgia, to wait out the war.

When the Union cavalry reached Solitude, they burned it to the ground.

Shadows on the Land

On Tuesday morning, December 2, 1862, the Union army began its march south just seven miles above Oxford. Days of rain and snow had turned much of the countryside to deep mud, making roads difficult to negotiate or altogether impassible, hindering both Confederate and Union armies in their movements. The rain, especially, reshaped vast reaches of eroded landscapes that melted and collapsed, covering roads and washing away whole hillsides, creating deep gorges that swallowed anything that tried to cross it. "Horses and riders went pell mell into the gorge," one observer wrote, "some never to come out." As the cavalry moved closer to the town, they were split into two wings, Colonel Grierson's Sixth Illinois Cavalry to the west near Wyatt, where Sherman was advancing, and the First Cavalry Brigade, commanded by Colonel A.L. Lee, comprising the Fourth Illinois Cavalry, Seventh Kansas, Second Iowa and the Third Michigan Cavalry commanded by Major Mizner.

Lee had the distinction of leading the First Brigade that would capture Oxford. Their orders were to advance down the Holly Springs Road into Oxford, then proceed south toward Coffeyville as far as the Yalobusha River, securing roads, bridges and rail line as he went. Lee anticipated strong resistance, but as he neared the town, he found only the occasional potshot coming from the woods. That changed a mile out of town. Suddenly beyond the woods to his right came sharp reports from all along the distant hills. Lee knew it was Mizner's Third Michigan Cavalry, traveling parallel to his own brigade, likely encountering the first Confederate line of defense along the northwestern perimeter of the town. Before he knew it, shots from the surrounding woods rang out in force, peppering Lee's own columns with a hail of bullets. Thinking he had run into the extended line of defense the Third Michigan had encountered, Lee deployed his troops into defensive positions and returned fire. In an effort to determine its strength, he deployed troops of the Seventh Kansas along the Confederate line he faced. But as it turned out, it was a separate force of lesser strength made up of troops of the Second Texas, Forty-third Mississippi and Second Tennessee Infantry, probably fewer than two thousand in number stretched out thin along the northern east–west town perimeter. Lee acted quickly, engaging the Confederates with sufficient firepower to break their lines and cause them to retreat into town. The Union cavalry, confident they had routed an inferior Confederate force, suddenly raced down North Street toward the square in the belief that the rebels had completely fled. Civilians in their homes watched in amazement and fear as the blue-coated Yankees thundered past their front yards toward the square. For many, the presence of blue coats in Oxford was the end of the world.

At William Turner's home, Jacob Thompson sat high atop the roof, field glasses in hand, watching the Yankees as they came. When the galloping blue uniforms streamed past Jefferson Street, he watched them as they collided headlong with a re-formed Confederate line of defense along Jackson and Depot Streets. Sheets of lead flew up into the Union columns, felling troopers and wounding others and causing Lee's men to scramble and retreat back up the street in surprised haste and confusion. Thompson, still observing the action from Turner's roof, suddenly felt a minie ball whirr by his head. Dropping his field glasses, he saw a lone Union cavalryman astride his horse recock his Sharps carbine and aim it for a second shot. Thompson jumped through a trapdoor in the roof just as the second round splintered the railing behind him. Bounding down the steps, he raced in panic, revolver in hand, until he came to and burst through the back door of the house at a full run. Leaping onto his horse, he galloped off and disappeared through the smoke and trees. Simultaneously, elements of the First Brigade were deployed to attack both flanks of the Confederate line, and after a short engagement, the Texas, Mississippi and Tennessee troops broke ranks and fled through the square and kept going.

By evening, as the moon came up over the quiet groves of oak and cedar, Oxford, Mississippi, was in Union hands.

CHAPTER 6

THE LAST GALLANT RUSH

"The army did all it could…it responded to the call nobly and cheerfully, and though it did not win a victory, it conquered a success."
—Robert E. Lee, commanding general, Army of Northern Virginia

General Ulysses S. Grant, Union commander of the Army of the Tennessee, entered a mostly deserted Oxford, Mississippi, on December 5, 1862. Like a modern Alexander the Great, he rode down North Street past the stately residences of Thomas Pegues, Augustus Longstreet, William Turner and others and was intrigued by what he found. In some of the houses, Union officers found tables still set for dinner, napkins on the table and glasses still filled with wine. In others, oil lamps were left burning, clothing was laid out on the beds and coals still smoldered in the fireplaces. In the square, stores still had coffee pots sitting on the shelves and at Neilsen's store shoes still sat on tables where they had been left. The square had become a city of canvas, shelter halves and wall tents crammed into the wrought-iron enclosure that surrounded the lone building at its center. Above them, presiding helpless over the scene of conquest was the Lafayette County Courthouse, its windows shot out during the battle, its facade riddled with damage, windows flung wide open and curtains hanging out, wet from rain.

Grant ordered that his staff officers be billeted in the best homes in town. For his own headquarters, the Union commander chose the abandoned, two-story, brick home of wealthy planter James Brown, situated on Depot Street (now Jackson Avenue) just a block from the railroad station and telegraph

Major General Ulysses S. Grant. In December 1862, Grant personally searched Jacob Thompson's home. Despite the initial damage done during the taking of Oxford, Grant quickly had order restored. *Courtesy of Library of Congress.*

office, a position that was ideally suited for monitoring Union communications and supply lines. But from the moment he hung up his sword belt in his new headquarters, Grant heard nothing but reports and complaints about the looting, pillaging and violence done by his men as they captured the town. Such activities, he knew, were not a part of any official army policy but rather the result of young, undisciplined soldiers out of control.

Since the beginning of the war, Grant and Sherman both had always restricted troops from damaging civilian property. In the first year of the war, looting, pillaging and plundering were never viewed by the majority of Civil War commanders as a military necessity. Regarding the treatment of civilians, Sherman and Grant shared the same views. Sherman, in particular, acted with considerable restraint, prohibiting his armies from any form of plundering of civilian property. Defending himself against an accusation by U.S. senator James Guthrie for improperly arresting and detaining civilians, Sherman replied that he "would not let our men burn fence rails for fire or gather fruit or vegetable though hungry." He further insisted that his forces were "tied by a deep-seated reverence for law and property." Yet as 1862 wore on, attitudes toward "reverence for law and property" began to change dramatically. The so-called "rose water" policy toward civilians, predicated on the assumption that the war had been caused by a minority of elite slave owners and political extremists and not by the general population, was cast aside in favor of one designed to punish and demoralize Southern society uniformly. Sherman reminded Senator Guthrie that "The rebels first introduced terror as part of their system," noting that while his own Union army had all along observed the conventions of war regarding respect of civilian property, the Confederates routinely violated those conventions, burning bridges, farms and personal property to keep them from falling into Yankee hands.

THE RAPE OF OXFORD

On the morning of December 6, Grant awoke to a delegation of the women of the town waiting in his parlor. They had braved the cold and rain to call upon the Union general in an effort to air their grievances about atrocities that had been committed in their town by his soldiers. They were not impressed by the figure that came out to meet them. Grant, who was just five-foot, seven-inches tall, was an unassuming figure who smoked cigars and rarely spoke. Dressed in a private's tunic and muddied boots, he looked more like a peasant than the general of a great army. While he was aware all along that looting had taken place, the ladies made him uncomfortably aware that his men had no discipline or morality, and as the morning wore on, more civilians arrived with even wilder stories that painted a picture of an army that was largely out of control. Grant knew that the bulk of the looting and destruction could be attributed to young, exuberant soldiers; still, it meant a general lack of discipline, and after listening to the long litany of complaints, he afterward ensured that order was restored.

While some in the press corps reported the destruction as "but few outrages," other correspondents told it like it was: "They took corn and chickens and all that could be eaten," wrote one correspondent. Other observers noted that Union soldiers had "entered houses and committed depredations, stealing money and other valuables." Chickens and fowl were stolen and slaughtered wholesale. "Dey kilt all our chickens an' turkeys," complained one slave. Former slave Rebecca Wood recalled years later, "the whole yard wuz full of chicken heads, but nary a chicken." Sarah Isom, wife of Dr. Isom, apprehended Grant one evening in back of William Turner's house and gave the general an earful about his soldiers who broke into her home and accosted her and her fourteen-year-old daughter, Mary. She demanded a guard to protect her family and her property, and Grant complied, sending her home with two armed Union infantrymen.

While the looting and atrocities were caused by a broad cross section of Union soldiers, the vast majority of accounts point to the men of the

The Lafayette County Courthouse during the Union occupation of December 1862. Troops are encamped on the south lawn of the courthouse as Grant's supply train slips past. (Note the broken glass in most of the upstairs windows.) This view is from the southwest corner of the square. *Courtesy of Special Collections, University of Mississippi Libraries.*

Seventh Kansas. In her diary, William S. Neilsen's wife wrote, "The Seventh Kansas Jayhawkers camped in our yard and garden and occupied part of our house. Killed nearly all our fowl, took all my meat, potatoes, nearly a barrel of molasses, all the meal, destroyed nearly 500 bushels of corn, burned the plank off the crib, the palings off the garden and yard fences, took all the fodder we had, took jars of butter, milk jars, pans, cups, coffee pots, sheets, towels, hoes, two carving knives, cooking vessels and a great many little things." The Pegueses, who had taken refuge in cousin Thomas's house at the end of North Street, seemed not to be able to escape the devastation either. "They broke into Thomas' cellar and destroyed everything," wrote daughter Ella Pegues to her son in the army. "Many articles of furniture, glass, and crockery were broken; the carriage and buggy hauled off; all his mules, horses, oxen, sheep, hogs, etc—killed…the plantation is a complete wreck."

Yet, the occupation had its stranger—and lighter—moments. One Union officer remembered seeing a cavalryman stagger away from a home carrying a grandfather clock. When asked what on earth he planned to do with it, the trooper explained he was going to take it apart and use the little gears for spur rowels. After that, all the grandfather clocks in town mysteriously disappeared. When one woman saw a familiar face among the Union soldiers guarding the town, she approached him and realized he had been a childhood neighbor and playmate back in Virginia before the war. Approaching the soldier, she called out his name and, after exchanging a few brief pleasantries, asked, "What are you doing here?" The young man, looking down at himself, turned beet red and sheepishly replied, "Guess I'm in the wrong uniform."

Some of the more harrowing reports of encounters with the Jayhawkers took place on the university campus. "I shall never forget our horror," Dr. E.W. Hilgard remembered years later. "We looked out of the little window in the upstairs of the observatory…and saw a lot of wild devils…with long blue army coats flying behind them, tall peaked hats on their heads, and each one flourishing at arms length a bright new tin coffee pot stolen from some store in Oxford." Hilgard watched them as they broke into the Lyceum, destroyed the dispensary stores and equipment and left destruction in their wake. At the observatory building, which was occupied by the families of Mr. Burton Harrison, Dr. Quinche and Dr. Hilgard, Harrison's daughter remembered how the Jayhawkers "burst into the main door, and spread themselves all over the building, breaking up apparatus and chemicals, and then rushing into the dwelling apartments, frightening us women nearly to death. Fortunately, however, they had not gone very far in their course when some officers arrived on the spot and fairly clubbed them into obedience in their orders to get back to camp."

AGENTS AND ABETTORS

Of all the homes in Oxford, Ulysses S. Grant had the most interest in the one belonging to the former interior secretary, Jacob Thompson. In September 1862, Secretary of War Edwin Stanton issued a series of general orders that set in motion a sweeping policy designed to find and apprehend persons involved in treasonable or disloyal practices against the federal government. Federal provost-marshals were appointed, and authority to detain and arrest individuals filtered down to military commanders in the field. They were authorized by whatever means they chose to "suppress the insurrection existing in the United States," and detain persons "from giving aid and comfort in various ways to the insurrection." Within these definitions, Stanton compiled a list of "conspicuous secessionists," most of whom were former congressmen and senators from the Southern states now comprising the Confederate political leadership. Secession was viewed by many in the North as a conspiracy to overthrow the United States government prior to the war, and Stanton, in his position as war secretary, became obsessed with finding the evidence, convinced the Confederate political leadership and their agents had been behind it. By 1862, he was obsessed with finding and arresting Jefferson Davis, and at one point even considered having the Confederate president assassinated. Among those in Davis's circle whom Stanton suspected was former U.S. interior secretary, Jacob Thompson.

Grant, under orders from Stanton, inspected Jacob Thompson's home personally. The mansion had been heavily looted already by the time Grant arrived. As the Union commander walked through its rooms, he was impressed by the immensity and elegance of Thompson's home, its long, wide hallways, intricately carved staircases and immense dining room lined with French mirrors gilded in gold leaf. Kate Thompson and her servants had already fled, leaving the house exposed to the whims of invaders. The army had confiscated 190 bales of his cotton, searched his drawers and closets and cabinets and took whatever they wanted. Among the effects Grant took from the house were Thompson's personal papers from before the war, detailing his opinions on North–South relations, his thoughts on certain politicians and his views on secession. Among them was a copy of his letter to former president James Buchanan in which Thompson called Lincoln a "blunderer" while reaffirming the rights of Southern states to self-determination. "We have separated," the letter concluded, "and our separation is perpetual." That Thompson had left such important documents behind indicated the speed with which the Union forces had invaded north Mississippi. Like many Southern political leaders under Stanton's suspicious eye, Jacob Thompson was now considered a traitor. Grant collected all the papers he could and sent them to Stanton in Washington, who later had passages from them printed in the Northern newspapers.

But on the morning of December 21, Grant's stay in Oxford suddenly came to an end. In the middle of the night, Confederate cavalry had attacked the Union supply depot at Holly Springs, captured the garrison of fifteen hundred men of the Eighth Wisconsin Regiment and severed the Union supply line. Along the way, they pillaged munitions, food and supplies, then burnt the town to the ground and destroyed the rail and telegraph lines. Grant first suspected Nathan Bedford Forrest but was surprised to learn his loss was the work of a lesser commander named General Earl Van Dorn. Van Dorn's cavalry had been spotted in the weeks before at Pontotoc heading north, presumably to link up with Forrest who was known to be operating in the Jackson area. But despite the knowledge that a large Confederate cavalry force was on the move to their rear, neither Grant nor Eighth Wisconsin commander colonel Murphy made any preparations to protect the depot.

For Grant and Sherman, the attack demonstrated the impossibility of maintaining so long a supply line for an army on the move. At the time of the

Holly Springs raid, the Union supply line extended from its forward most position south of the Yalobusha, to Jackson, Tennessee, and extended even beyond to Columbus, Kentucky. Now he was without communications and provisions for nearly forty thousand troops. It was here at Oxford that Grant and Sherman came to realize the cumbersome futility of long supply trains, opting instead for the new solution of foraging and living off the resources of the land and its people wherever the army moved. Meanwhile, the news of the attack on Holly Springs caused a great deal of rejoicing and gloating among the people in Oxford.

Confederate general Earl Van Dorn, circa 1862. Unimpressive as a leader and in search of his own glory, his brilliant and daring attack on the Union supply depot at Holly Springs in 1862 completely surprised Grant, causing the Union general to retreat from northern Mississippi. *Courtesy of Library of Congress.*

Grant later wrote in his memoirs:

> *They came with broad smiles on their faces, indicating intense joy, to ask what I was going to do now without anything for my soldiers to eat. I told them that I was not disturbed; that I had already sent troops and wagons to collect all the food and forage they could find for fifteen miles on each side of the road. Countenances soon changed, and so did the inquiry. The next was, "What are WE to do?"*

Grant advised them to "emigrate east, or west, fifteen miles and assist in eating up what we left." The Union army, now crippled by the destruction of its supply line, withdrew back north to his previous position along the line of the Memphis to Charleston Railroad, foraging as it went. As Grant left town, he ordered the railroad depot and telegraphers office burned.

That winter would see starvation and destitution grip the population amid one of the coldest and snowiest winters in Oxford history.

INTO THE FRAY AT LAST

Meanwhile, the war in the East still raged, its leaders and men still caught in the grip of its violence, still clinging—despite fading hopes—to its cause for which companies like the University Greys, Lamar Rifles and Nineteenth Mississippi were formed. Long before Grant began moving south toward Oxford, Lieutenant Colonel Lucius Lamar, who had been staying at Augustus Longstreet's home, had recovered sufficiently from his attack of "apoplexy" to return to duty at the front. Still dragging his left leg slightly, he rejoined his regiment near Yorktown in March 1862, just as McClellan began his drive up the peninsula toward Richmond. In April, as the Nineteenth Mississippi pressed on toward Yorktown and the inevitable clash to come, he cheered his men on, giving occasional speeches to lift their spirits.

On May 5, the Battle of Williamsburg began, and Lamar at last took to the field of fire. Mott had divided the regiment into two wings, with Lamar in command of the right. Not long after the first volleys were fired, and as Lamar's right wing pressed forward against the Union line, he was informed that Mott had fallen and the command of the regiment was now his. Amid the smoke and confusion, he suddenly realized he had no idea where the left wing of the regiment was. At the same time, a huge gap had been created in the Confederate line, and as the Union infantry continued to press Lamar on his right flank, he halted his advance briefly to re-form his own forces. As he did so, he suddenly discovered the location of the left wing and moved quickly to rejoin with it. This he was able to do without much trouble, but once done, it strengthened his forces, which contributed directly to the Confederate effort to repulse McClellan's assault. It was a bold move, earning Lamar the admiration and commendations of Generals A.P. Hill, James Longstreet and George Pickett. The former fire-eater who never before quite comprehended military strategy suddenly had become quite the tactician. In the end, the Union offensive was stymied, and Johnston's army withdrew intact along the road toward the Chicahominy River and Richmond.

Battle had been a sobering experience for Lamar. In his report, he stated his regiment had suffered 25 percent casualties, including the loss of its commander, Colonel C.H. Mott, who fell on the field, shot through the heart. The manner of Lamar's actions won him high compliments from all the Confederate leadership that day, but he never allowed himself to think of his actions at Williamsburg as anything more than doing what was expected of him, and he downplayed the praise. Mott's death affected him greatly, and as he rode northwestward toward the Chickahominy, his life had changed forever. His own probable death likely began to weigh on his mind as he crossed the river to set up a line of defense and prepare for the next battle. And that was where his role as a rising battlefield commander ended. As he readied himself in camp for the next battle, he suffered another violent seizure. He was taken to Richmond, where he convalesced until June, then was sent back to Oxford for another rest and recovery.

When he saw Richmond again in early November 1862, his old friend Colonel James Chestnut barely recognized him. He was disheveled and haggard, and Chestnut's wife Mary found him "more absent-minded and distrait than ever." Whether a symptom of the apoplexy or the outcome of another process, Lamar was ill through most of 1863 and 1864. In addition to his own problems, his sister died and his brother, Thomas B. Lamar, had been killed in battle. Further, he worried that as Sherman's army pressed toward Atlanta, Union troops might invade Oxford, Georgia, where his wife, Virginia, was then staying with the Longstreets.

For the duration, Lucius Lamar was assigned to the military courts as a judge advocate. It was during this period that he began to shrug off the old self he had been and take on features of the new man he was to become. Somewhere among Richmond, Mott's death and the latest seizure, Lucius Lamar had crossed his own Rubicon. He now began struggling with the issues of death, fate and destiny through those precepts of Christian thought and spirituality he had never taken time to consider in the past. Perhaps he was trying to make genuine sense of the war, or of his difficulties in respect to the divine will, or perhaps it was merely his way of substituting faith for the pitiless fate he had been dealt. In any case, he wrote to his wife: "I am still trying to subordinate all worldly things to the considerations associated with eternity…the favor of God and the well-being of my soul hereafter. Pray to God, my darling, that we may all be his children."

THE STONE WALL

In the two years since their patriotic sendoff from the Oxford depot, battle after battle gradually thinned the ranks of the University Greys, Lamar Rifles, Pegues Defenders and many others, as classmate, neighbor, father, brother and friend fell one after another on the field of battle. Since First Manassas, the Greys and the Rifles had been engaged in one way or another at Seven Pines, Gaines Mills, Second Manassas, Sharpsburg, Fredericksburg and Chancellorsville. Gone from the uniforms were the bright red-ribboned fronts, the tall Hardee hats accented with polished brass and ostrich plumes; gone were the neat trousers, the new shoes and the slick, black leathers. In their stead were tired, grey uniforms muddied and soiled with the dirt of battle and the stench of sweat and death. Shoes were coming apart, shirts were worn through and trousers were shredded and torn in the seat and at the knees. Other resources were drying up as well: fewer reinforcements were being sent from Richmond, provisions were becoming more scarce, clothing and shoes were not replaced. To make do, soldiers of the Eleventh Mississippi begged, borrowed and stole what they needed from the local population; clothing, shoes and ammunition were even scavenged from the corpses of the battlefield dead. It had been a long time since Oxford.

Private Jonathan Clark's letter home expressed most sentiments among the soldiers: "I am really sick of the war and where is the man that is not?" Certainly not Jerrie Gage of the Greys, who, after receiving an aggravating wound at Gaines Mill, had been working for some time to secure himself a replacement so he could go home. "I am right glad that Irvin is about to succeed in getting me a substitute," he wrote to his sister on June 10, 1863. "I rejoiced to receive a telegram from him this morning stating that the boy is on his way." Sixteen-year-old Thomas Fondren McKie, who joined the Greys in March 1862, was writing a similar letter home. "Mother," he insisted, "I want you to write to President Davis to get me off. Say to him that I joined contrary to your will and that I am a minor…all the officers in our company advised me to do this." McKie hoped to follow home to Oxford his underage friend Billie Barr, whose mother had written to Davis and who was mustered out just weeks earlier. But Davis didn't release Tommie McKie, presumably because the Confederacy suddenly decided it could spare no more soldiers. By 1863, more and more underage youths were being accepted into the front ranks as Richmond struggled to win its declared Southern independence.

On June 3, 1863, Lee's Army of Northern Virginia began its march north from Fredericksburg toward what would ultimately become the final chapter in the history of the University Greys. Like a lumbering goliath, the Army of Northern Virginia moved behind the cover of the Blue Ridge mountains as Jeb Stuart's Cavalry kept the Army of the Potomac occupied, thus allowing Lee to move in relative secrecy. Marching in three separate columns, Longstreet, Ewell and Hill crossed into Pennsylvania by June 20. To be moving north was balm for the men of the Eleventh Mississippi. They were battle weary and dejected, but the invasion of Pennsylvania raised their hopes that Bobby Lee was finally on the offensive. Perhaps, they thought, this move would finally turn the tide of the war in favor of the Confederacy.

Few, however, expected the opportunity to "whoop the Yankees" to come as quickly on the heels of their enthusiasm as it did.

On July 1, as Lee's army moved north, elements of Heth's Third Corps unintentionally bumped into a company of Union cavalry commanded by Kentucky-born John Buford near a small town called Gettysburg. Neither side wanted a fight, but by 10:00 a.m., events conspired against both commanders as John F. Reynold's Union First Corps arrived on the field, dug in and deployed against Heth's men. Lee, upon hearing the exchange of gunfire several miles away, was profoundly disturbed that his orders to avoid engaging the enemy at all costs had not been obeyed. It was a necessary precaution, since General Stuart's Cavalry had not been heard from in days and Lee was effectively operating in the blind. "An army without cavalry in a strange and hostile country," wrote Major W.H. Taylor of Lee's staff, "is a man deprived of his eyesight." From seven miles away, the University Greys, marching along the road as the rear guard of a supply train near Cashtown, also heard the distant guns. By mid-afternoon, the Greys were deployed forward to rejoin A.P. Hill's Corps on the Confederate right wing, now straddling Chambersburg Pike on the western banks of Willoughby Run and facing Reynolds's Union First Corps. By nightfall, the Eleventh Mississippi helped push Reynolds back overtop Seminary Ridge to the other side of Emmitsburg Road on the south edge of Gettysburg.

Despite the uncertainty he felt from lack of Stuart's reconnaissance throughout most of the first day's fighting, Lee was generally pleased with the result, but deep down the Confederate commander remained in somewhat of a panic. He was convinced there was power behind the Federal force, but without Stuart's Cavalry, he had no idea where it was or how to measure it. His only option was to hurriedly bring up the rest of his forces and organize them for the conflict he knew was coming in the morning. The Eleventh Mississippi, meanwhile, tired and exhausted from the first day's fighting, was sent to the rear in reserve. There they would remain that night and for most of the next day. At the beginning of the war, the regiment had entered service with about 1,100 effectives; but by the time they came to Gettysburg, only 386 remained. Of the original 136 University Greys who enlisted, only 31 were present for duty on July 1, along with only 34 of the original 135 who enlisted in the Lamar Rifles.

On the night of July 2, the Eleventh was moved forward again and assigned to the brigade of General Joseph R. Davis, a nephew of Jefferson Davis. Most of the boys had heard about the brutal fighting the day before, which, they were told, had been withering and murderous, fought in places with names like the Devil's Den, Plum Run and the Valley of Death. The Third Corps, to which the Eleventh belonged, had been virtually destroyed and Caldwell's division was cut to pieces in the Wheat Field. The sounds of battle continued well after dark as the Eleventh moved up to their new position on the Confederate left and tried to settle in for the night.

Within the Greys's camp, Jerrie Gage and his childhood friend, Jim Dailey, sat together and stared at the fire, talking of home and Mississippi. A melancholy Gage had hoped the replacement he was assured would come might have arrived before he had to go into another battle; he still limped badly from the wound to his hip he received at Gaines Mill, and he had to try and survive this one. But he remained optimistic. Surely after this battle, his replacement would find him, and he could muster out at last. He looked forward to making it home in time to help with the summer chores before harvest like he did before the war. He would see his kid sister again, as well as his girlfriend. But above all, the first thing he resolved to do when he finally made it home—when he walked through that familiar front door of the family home—would be to kiss his mother and hold her tight. He had promised her he would come home and he wanted to keep that promise. Jerrie Gage, like so many soldiers who were battle weary and worn out, just wanted it to end. Before long, the campfire he and Dailey sat before had gone out and the men uneasily tried to sleep.

The morning of July 3 dawned misty, with fog lingering in patches on the field and among the trees, the acrid smell of gunpowder, fires and dead corpses still hung in the air, its peculiar stench inescapable. Today was, Jerrie Gage thought hopefully, the last battle he would ever have to fight. The morning passed with fighting on Culp's Hill and elsewhere, while Pettigrew, Trimble and Pickett's divisions remained at the ready on Seminary Ridge. At half past one o'clock in the afternoon, Confederate gunners pulled the lanyards on two Napoleon cannon. It was the signal to begin a planned artillery barrage against the Union line in an effort to soften it up in preparation for a massive final assault. The whole crest of ridges sent screaming, whistling death into the air as hundreds of Confederate cannon belched fire with a ferocity that made the ground tremble in fear of man. In front of Pettigrew's division alone, sixty-nine cannon fired a continuous stream of shot, canister and shell, falling in fearful arcs through the deadly sky, exploding above the blue ranks in horrendous detonations, throwing shells and hot fragments into men—killing, maiming and wounding. The Confederate bombardment showered enough projectiles, shells, shot, canister and sheets of fire to rank it as the largest artillery barrage of the war. Union commander Winfield

Scott Hancock even called it "the heaviest artillery fire I have ever known." Hancock then ordered a return barrage.

What sailed back across the skies above Emmitsburg Road from Union guns suddenly began pelting the Confederate lines with the same merciless fire they had been receiving. In the divisions of Pickett, Trimble and Pettigrew, shells fell on men like rain, the ground shaking and trees shuddering beneath from the impact of solid shot, detonating shells and the galling explosions above their heads. One Virginian observed that "it seemed that death was in every foot of space." Colonel Francis M. Green of the Eleventh Mississippi ordered his men to lie down flat to wait out the barrage. Private Hugh Bridges remembered seeing Jerrie Gage still sitting up just as a large shell whistled downward and exploded in front of them. Gage immediately called out that he'd been hit. Rushing over, Hugh Bridges was stunned by the damage done. One shell fragment ripped across Gage's shoulder, almost tearing away his left arm below the socket, while another raked across his abdomen, laying open much of his viscera and tearing away part of his pelvis.

Jim Dailey, who that day was assigned as a litter bearer to the regimental field hospital, along with Bridges, bundled the wounded Gage onto a makeshift canvas litter and dragged him to the rear, where he was put on a table and examined by Dr. Joseph Holt, assistant surgeon of the Second Mississippi.

"How long have I to live?" Gage struggled to ask.

"A very few hours," came the reply.

"Then let me die easy," he pleaded. "I would do the same for you."

"I will see to it," Holt reassured him. The surgeon called for a two-ounce bottle of "black drop," a concentrated mixture of opium. He poured a tablespoonful into a cup of water and mixed it. Before giving it to him, he thought to ask, "Have you a message for anyone?"

"My mother," he groaned. "I want to write." Holt quickly sat him up and helped him as he scribbled a last, desperate note on a piece of blue writing paper. Then, pressing the paper into his wounds and staining it with his own blood, he gave it to Holt to send home. After that, the surgeon gave him the black drop mixture, and Jerrie Gage drifted off into a sleep from which he would never wake up.

About twenty minutes after the Union guns fell silent, the brigades, battalions, and divisions at last rose to their feet in one motion and advanced beyond the trees into the bright sunshine. The Eleventh Mississippi, assigned to Pettigrew's division, was formed up on the far left of Davis's brigade; to their immediate left was Mayo's brigade of Virginians, making up the extreme left flank of Lee's line. As they peered across the open field still saturated

By the end of the war's second year, an older and more war-weary Jeremiah Gage sat for the camera in his University Greys uniform. Suffering from a painful hip wound received at the Battle of Gaines Mills, he sought a substitute who would be willing to take his place in the regiment. In June 1863, as Jeremiah received word that a replacement was on his way, General Lee took the Army of Northern Virginia into Pennsylvania. *Courtesy of Special Collections, University of Mississippi Libraries.*

with smoke and death, the boys at last saw the magnitude of what was to be required of them. As if by theater, with swords held high, orders chimed out, repeated down the line in perfect coordination, then the swords fell forward and the grey lines moved steadily toward the Union lines, three brigades under Pickett to the south and six to the north under Trimble and Pettigrew. They marched forward to the cadence of the fifes, flags flying in the light breeze that had come up, marching through high grass almost without thought or fear anymore. Their objective was a stone wall on the other side of Emmitsburg Road. Out in front, a Union skirmisher described the scene simply as "a glittering forest of bayonets," while a Union colonel watched in amazement, recalling that they "seemed impelled by some irresistible force." In the front ranks of the Greys marched Frank O. Dailey, William R. Hall, James Ballard, William Raines, Thomas Heslep, Joseph L. McKie and his sixteen-year-old cousin, Thomas Fondron McKie.

In the ensuing lull that the scene created, the Union gunners and infantry waited patiently, watching the Confederates come. Pettigrew's Division moved steadily onward down through the valley to the slight dip about halfway, then advanced up across the field, dappled by moving cloud shadows and sunshine. One soldier noted the texture of the slope was "covered with clover as soft as a Turkish carpet." Ahead they could see the stone wall reaching left to right and behind it a sea of blue. Colonel Mayo's brigade of Virginians, who had been badly beaten up at Chancellorsville and whose morale was almost nonexistent by this time, looked ahead and could see the Union gunners sighting their cannon on them. Suddenly the magnitude of their situation seemed to hit them. Barely two hundred yards before reaching Emmitsburg Road, the entire brigade "had become as still and thoughtful as Quakers at a love feast." Then in an instant, Mayo's entire brigade broke and ran for the rear, leaving Davis's men suddenly exposed on the left to the Union gunners. Francis M. Green, now colonel of the Eleventh, knew there was no turning back for any of them; the only way home was over that wall and through the sea of blue, and they would have to fight and kill every last Yankee to get there. As the thick lines of grey crossed Emmitsburg Road, they continued up the slope toward the wall. "C'mon, Johnny! Keep on comin'!" one Union gunner shouted. And come they did, marching in step to the fifes, the ranks dressed perfectly down the line, a two-and-a-half-mile-wide formation of grey. The Union gunners watched and listened in amazement to the "rustle of thousands of feet amid stubble," and the "murmur and jingle" of legs and equipment as it came. When Pettigrew and Pickett's Divisions got to within fifty yards of the stone wall, hundreds of cannon opened up and fired into their ranks.

All at once, a fearful moan rose into the air as whole regiments just disappeared. Huge gaps opened up in the Confederate ranks. The Eleventh lost both its field officers and all of its captains. Stumbling forward, pounded by the sheets of fire from Union guns and gnawed at by rifle fire, it was all the Greys and Rifles could do to stay on their feet and keep the flags from going down. Men on both sides screamed and yelled, firing into the smoke, swearing, stabbing with bayonets and flailing murderously away at anything that moved. It all combined to produce a sound someone later described as "strange and terrible, a sound that came from thousands of human throats, yet was not a commingling of shouts and yells, but rather like a vast mournful roar." Tommie McKie looked around in the smoke and saw no one he recognized. The officers were gone; the sergeants were gone. He heard someone yell, "Follow me!" Then a few remaining men around him rushed forward through the smoke toward the stone wall, no longer as a unit, but as individuals in one last gallant rush through a withering hail of rifle and musket fire. On reaching the wall, one soldier hiked up and went over and disappeared. Others tried to follow but never made it. One Union officer later wrote in his diary that the Rebels "fell like wheat before the garner." But it was a regimental surgeon who stated the grim reality of it: "It looked like murder."

Confederate dead on the plains of Gettysburg near where the Eleventh Mississippi passed into history. *Courtesy of Library of Congress.*

One of the Eleventh's privates managed to plant the colors on the stone wall, and a spare few managed even to breech the line, now just single dots of grey in a sea of blue. They were all quickly cut down by Union infantry or obliterated out of existence by a single cannon blast. The killing lasted only a little while longer, and then it was all over. As the din of battle subsided in the pale light of that July afternoon, nothing would ever be the same again for either side. The Eleventh Mississippi Regiment suffered 87 percent casualties, the highest casualty rate of any regiment during the war, North or South. The University Greys suffered 100 percent casualties: out of 31 men who went into battle, 14 were killed and 17 wounded. At least 13 of the wounded were captured and became prisoners of war. On July 3, 1863, the University Greys ceased to exist as a fighting unit.

Sixteen-year-old Tommie Fondren McKie had made it all the way to the stone wall before he was cut down. His lifeless body was found after the battle the next morning lying at the base of the stone wall and was later buried among his fellow soldiers in a mass grave.

CHAPTER 7

THE VANQUISHED

"Above the smoke and stir of this dim spot which men call earth."
—*Virgil,* The Aeneid

For the first time in his life, Jacob Thompson wasn't sure what he was going to do. The war had brought a vengeful chaos and disruption upon his world of northern Mississippi, making it a place he hardly knew any longer. Hundreds of residents had taken the oath of allegiance to the Union during Grant's occupation, which gave rise to the existence of spies and informants in the county, capable of turning in even old friends who were wanted by the authorities. Oxford, once a patriotic community of proud people, had become a town of contradictions, with residents whose only motivation now was their own grim survival.

To avoid possible detection, Thompson rode into town under cover of night in the early spring of 1863. What he found both frustrated and angered him as nothing else ever had. The wanton destruction of property in the square and among the surrounding homes was infuriating. He visited Sarah Isom, who lived on Jefferson Street, and listened to her descriptions of the destruction at the hands of Union troops. He also talked to Rebecca Pegues, still living at her cousin Thomas's home at the far end of North Street, and William Turner, William S. Neilsen and a number of others who escaped Grant's occupation with their lives. They all told a similar story.

But it wasn't until he returned to his own house that the impact of what had happened hit home. His beautiful Home Place, which he and Kate had built and which had been the center of their world for twenty-three years, was reduced to a dark, desolate shell of broken windows, heaps of scattered dirt and shattered china, graffiti-strewn bedrooms and revolting piles of garbage and debris left in the hallways. The violation of it struck him deeply. When he came to his private, two-room study and discovered that all of his personal papers had been taken, he at last began to understand the scope of the Union war effort: that it had broadened beyond mere military goals to espionage, intrigue and even character assassination. Later, when the publishing of his private papers by Edwin M. Stanton in Northern newspapers attempted to frame Thompson's prewar thinking as "treasonous," it further aggravated an already festering wound. What Stanton had done, he felt, was beyond the boundaries of decency. The game had become a dirty one, a new kind of propaganda warfare based on misperception, lies and subterfuge aimed at nothing less than destroying human beings. The war was no longer a matter of honor and cause and right; it was now a desperate battle waged in the shadow lands against a relentless leviathan Thompson was sadly convinced would eventually consume the South and ultimately destroy it. The end, he came to believe, was only a matter of time.

But then in April 1864, he received a letter from Jefferson Davis requesting that he come to the Confederate capital. Davis expressed to Thompson his worry about the course of the war. With the defeats at Gettysburg and Vicksburg and with Sherman on the move pressing Joseph E. Johnston's army into retreat toward Atlanta, the president was desperate. The Confederate Congress had recently created the Special and Secret Bureau of the War Department—in effect the Confederate Secret Service—and Davis felt Jacob Thompson was the man to lead it. But first, he wanted to try and open up secret negotiations with the North, extending diplomatic overtures of peace between both sides in the hope of perhaps bringing about a cease-fire or even a peaceful end to the hostilities. Davis suggested the neutral turf of Canada was the best arena for such negotiations and proposed that if the peace talks failed, Thompson would then be authorized to conduct clandestine operations against the North as he saw fit. Still bearing the mental scars of the destruction he had witnessed in Oxford, Jacob Thompson accepted the position. In early May 1864, he set out for Toronto, sailing through the blockade to Bermuda, then north to Canada. In his satchel was an estimated $600,000 in gold and Federal paper currency from the Confederate government.

Upon arrival in Toronto, Thompson began making overtures to prominent Northern businessmen and politicians that the South was ready to talk. But while he may have had grand visions of perhaps being the man to help bring the desired end to a bloody civil war, his diplomatic efforts were, nonetheless, a failure. The North had no interest in talks. The setback only seemed to reinforce Thompson's resolve to proceed even more vigorously to his next and most discordant role—that of chief of the Confederate Secret Service. His operating plan called specifically for creating havoc in the North through disruption of the market economy, causing fragmentation of Northern state alliances through secession initiatives, destroying the North's manufacturing base, liberating Confederate prisoners from Northern prisons and burning cities and towns so as to induce general panic.

He was quickly introduced to an organization called the Sons of Liberty, a pro-South movement then operating throughout the northern United States. Military in its operations but political in its objectives, it held that individual states were sovereign, had the right of secession and that the general government had no authority to coerce a seceding state. With Thompson's financial assistance, the Sons of Liberty planned to take advantage of the uncertain political conditions inherent in the upcoming 1864 election and cause a general uprising in the states of Illinois, Indiana and Ohio. That effort failed, when arms procured for the uprising were discovered in Indianapolis and the agents involved were arrested.

Thompson's next effort involved freeing the Confederate prisoners on Johnson's Island, one of the Union's most notorious prison camps. This was his chance to plan what was essentially a military operation: to surveil the island, mount an assault, take the island and free the prisoners. Confederate captain Charles Cole became the man Thompson chose to lead the operation. But that plan also failed when Cole was arrested by federal agents on a tip just as he was about to pirate the steamer *Michigan*. Ironically, Captain Cole became a prisoner on the island he set out to liberate.

It didn't take long for Union detectives and spies to discover Thompson's operations, which were run out of the Queen's Hotel in Toronto. Thompson, although a skilled national politician and businessman, was naive and indiscreet about his activities in Toronto, and was clearly the wrong man to head a spy operation. Soon, it was nearly impossible for anyone to come or go from Toronto without being detected by Union spies. In one famous incident, two of Thompson's operatives, Captain Robert Kennedy and Lieutenant John Ashbrook, taking an urgent message from their chief to Jefferson Davis in Richmond became the objects of just such intrigue. Traveling separately on the train from Toronto to Detroit, Ashbrook turned around at one point to see two Union detectives apprehend Kennedy, then look forward as if to locate Ashbrook. Thinking fast, Ashbrook opened a window, threw one leg out, ducked his head and jumped into the darkness. While Ashbrook eventually made it to Richmond, Kennedy was not so lucky: he was tried and hanged as a spy in April 1865.

As 1864 wore on, failures like the Kennedy and Ashbrook affair happened with increasing frequency. Jacob Thompson's operations in Canada fell into complete disarray by the early spring of 1865. His undercover operatives were quickly identified, caught and jailed; his comings and goings from his hotel were recorded in minute detail from the train station across the street. Even Canadian authorities, angry at Thompson's disregard for the country's neutrality, threatened to jail him. Indeed, Thompson's life in Toronto ultimately became a cat-and-mouse game played out in shadows, not knowing from one minute to the next who to trust and who to betray. In a December 1864 letter to Confederate secretary of war Judah P. Benjamin, Thompson himself lamented the limitations inherent in the spy business. "I had hoped to have accomplished more," he wrote. "But the bane and curse of this country is the surveillance under which we act. Detectives or those ready to give information, stand on every corner."

In the end, Jacob Thompson discovered that he had traitors in his inner circle all along, feeding a continuous stream of information on his activities to federal authorities back in Washington. In his War Department office, Edwin Stanton read all the detailed reports sent to him about Thompson, Davis and the Southern leadership, perhaps with a view that as the war approached its ultimate conclusion, there would come the time to prosecute those who had caused it. As Atlanta fell to Sherman that November and as he began his march to toward Savannah and the sea, the end Thompson saw coming was at last upon them.

The End of the World

In northern Mississippi, Oxford languished for more than a year as Confederate cavalry hit and sparred with Union forces in continuing operations aimed to restore some semblance of order and reestablish a defensive line. In most people's minds, the mere presence of Nathan Bedford Forrest's Cavalry in the region was seen as a great hope that the Yankees might still be destroyed or driven off. In June, Forrest's thirty-five hundred man force scored a decisive victory against an eighty-five hundred man Union force commanded by Samuel D. Sturgis at Bryce's Crossroads. In response to the continuing threat of Forrest's Cavalry, Union forces under General Andrew Jackson Smith set out from Memphis by train to Grand Junction with non-specific orders to find and destroy the Confederates, specifically Nathan Bedford Forrest. From Grand Junction, Smith chose to march South through Holly Springs toward Oxford, where Forrest was known to garrison his men and horses. His reconnaissance indicated Forrest had been at Pontotoc a few days before and was now headed west to Oxford. Knowing he had superior numbers, Smith knew it would not be long before he found his quarry.

With elements of the Sixteenth and Seventeenth Corps comprising infantry and cavalry of nearly fourteen thousand effectives, Smith doggedly headed south along the same line of

General Andrew Jackson Smith. In later years, he never talked about why he burned Oxford. Scholars agree no military necessity dictated it nor was there any other reason for Smith to occupy the town except the premeditated purpose of burning it. *Courtesy of Library of Congress.*

approach he had followed with Grant in 1862. Days of rain had reduced the roads to ankle-deep mud with streams swollen beyond their banks, making it nearly impossible to move. But once more, the Confederates were waiting for the Yankees at the Tallahatchie River, and for two days after they remained engaged, repelling any Union advance across the river with blistering resistance. Smith's solution was to sidestep the Confederates and force a crossing above Abbeville on August 7. But here his forces met with an even heavier Confederate resistance, which he learned were comprised of lesser elements of Forrest's own cavalry. The encounter turned into a protracted, two-day skirmish along Hurricane Creek that gave Forrest's main force distance from the Union army. But where was the rebel leader headed? To find out, Smith deployed scouts and cavalry to reconnoiter. One of those he sent was a newly promoted brigadier general, Edward Hatch of the Second Iowa Cavalry. His orders were to proceed south to Oxford to determine enemy presence and strength. On the outskirts of town, Hatch ran into Confederate skirmishers, but realized quickly it was only a small force of infantry defending the town. Ordering up his guns, he commenced to send shell and canister directly into the Confederate infantry, quickly dispersing them into the woods. Then, as a precaution, he decided to shell the town itself to reduce any further possible resistance.

Confederate cavalry loitering on the balcony of Avent's Bank first heard whistling, and then as the shells hit and exploded in the square, the men scattered, running and falling over themselves to get away. Confederate captain Bright was in such a hurry, he failed to untie his horse's lead rein, causing both horse and rider to come crashing down as he pulled away from the hitching post. Columns of blue once more streamed down North Street toward the square. One resident noted it was a repeat of 1862 with soldiers indiscriminately looting, pillaging, robbing and destroying everything in their path. It was, another resident noted, "like a plague of locusts descending on a wheat field."

With the Union troops occupying Oxford, the home of Jacob Thompson once again became the object of Union scrutiny. In addition to reconnoitering for rebel presence, Hatch's only other action was to ride with a mounted detachment directly to the Thompson home. Kate Thompson was ill at the time and her daughter-in-law, Sallie was bedridden upstairs after having just delivered a baby. Barging into the home, he moved from room to room against Kate's protests, searching the cupboards, sideboards and bedrooms, while his officers again searched Jacob's offices in the rear. Apparently satisfied, he ordered a wagon brought up, which he filled with the Thompson's furniture, china, silver and bedding items. Then he departed, riding north out of town to rejoin Smith. His report, combined with the cavalry scouts, confirmed that Forrest had departed Oxford already and headed in a westerly direction toward Memphis. That the Union army had encountered a smaller contingent of Forrest's cavalry along the Tallahatchie meant the rebel leader had split his force in two. Meanwhile, it was reported that Confederate general Chalmers had moved south across the Yocona River.

With Forrest moving west, Smith unexplainably ordered his entire cavalry to head south and advance once again upon Oxford. He arrived unopposed at just after eight o'clock on the morning of August 22, 1864. Residents watched as Union troops spread quickly throughout the town. The Union general himself, according to some reports, appeared to be well intentioned toward the inhabitants, selecting certain homes and posting guards on them, then sending out reconnaissance patrols to secure the perimeter of the town. Then calling his officers together, he laid out his plan for what was to be done, each subordinate acknowledging it and departing to take up his position. By midmorning, the Union general rode out to the Thompson home, where he quickly surveyed the interior of the house, then ordered Kate Thompson and all other occupants out. Soldiers had to carry the still bedridden Sallie Thompson out through the front door and deposit her on the lawn. Kate was forced outside as well, grabbing at the few keepsakes as she was hustled out onto the lawn. After a quick survey of the details, Smith simply ordered it put to the torch. Joanna Isom, one of Jacob Thompson's house servants who was seven at the time, remembered that Smith and his men rode away "whoopin' an' hollerin' an' singin.'" As the fire spread, someone thought to run inside and rescue Sallie's baby before the flames engulfed the house entirely. By two o'clock, it began to rain. Kate Thompson, Sallie and the baby, along with Joanna, her mother Amy, and the rest of the servants, could only stand by helpless and watch in stunned amazement as the fiery destruction did its work.

Arriving back in the square, Smith was hastily handed a dispatch informing him that Nathan Bedford Forrest had raided and heavily damaged the Union supply depot at Memphis. According to some accounts, Smith's manner changed at that moment into an even darker mood, and it was then—some say in revenge for Forrest's raid—that he ordered the town torched. Yet his decision to move his forces on Oxford in the first place when he already knew Forrest was headed west suggests he had another motive for coming to Oxford. No military necessity dictated it nor was there any other reason for Smith to occupy the town except a premeditated purpose of burning it. The dispatch, which certainly left him red-faced, only served to aggravate the Union general; it did not reflect well on him or his superiors that he had let the rebel commander slip through his fingers to make such a raid. Yet by the time the dispatch arrived, Smith's work was largely done. He recalled the guards he had placed on the homes he had previously selected and then simultaneously pulled back the cavalry that secured the town perimeter. It was then he issued the order to begin the burning.

While some accounts describe soldiers scurrying helter-skelter like demons setting the town ablaze, many describe a much more ordered process in which Smith personally supervised the torching of specific structures. The private homes he selected for burning, in almost every case, were those of prominent secessionists, political leaders and wealthy planters. The businesses on the square, however, were indiscriminately torched. The courthouse was set

Vanquished Oxford. According to evidence in Union and Confederate accounts, there appeared to be no need for federal troops to occupy Oxford on August 22, 1864, except for the express purpose of burning it. *Courtesy of Special Collections, University of Mississippi Libraries.*

alight, as was Mrs. Butler's Oxford Inn and Avent's Bank, Neilsen's Mercantile and the Masonic Hall. The carpentry and blacksmith shops, the newspaper and liquor stores, along with a number of the finer homes around the square were set on fire. On Depot Street, the home of James Brown, which served as Grant's headquarters, was consumed by flames, as was the home of Dr. Henry Branham next door. By 4:00 p.m. Smith's work was done. Collecting his forces, he rode past the burnt foundation of the train depot, then turned northwest onto the Memphis Road and disappeared into the night.

In his wake the Union army left the burnt skeleton of Oxford along with a wasteland that was once the proud and prosperous landscape of Lafayette County. "We are a subjugated people," wrote a defeated Rebecca Pegues in June 1865. "Humiliated to the dust." What the Yankees left held no further military significance for either army, and no other battles or skirmishes happened there. From August 1864 until Appomattox, the white residents who remained in Oxford were confronted by a barren, empty, desolate purgatory of broken dreams and tortured, tideless grief. They dug up the silver, groveled for scraps and ate what they could to keep from starving. The more than five thousand former slaves were left to the reality of their freedom and the confusing tide of blessings and dangers it wrought. Soon the soldiers, who years before departed Oxford in gloried optimism and patriotic pageantry, began at last to make their way back along the roads in weary procession, like pale, fallen leaves carried adrift on the currents of a summer stream. There were no drums or fifes to march to, no shiny brass buttons or swords to glitter boldly in the sun. Only the vanquished remained, left only to their memories of who they once were and confronted by the enigma of what they had become.

CHAPTER 8

THE EVER SOUNDING MURMUR OF GOD

"And now, young gentlemen, as you go home I pray that you may have prosperity and happiness through life, with just enough sorrow to remind you that this earth is not your home."
—Lucius Quintus Cincinnatus Lamar, June 27, 1865

On April 27, 1874, a newly reelected Democratic congressman Lucius Lamar stood among a packed House of Representatives and delivered a eulogy of former Massachusetts senator Charles Sumner, the leading Senate Radical who had just died. "Strange as, in looking back upon the past, the assertion may seem," he began, "impassible as it would have been ten years ago to make it...Mississippi regrets the death of Charles Sumner, and sincerely unites in paying homage to his memory." From the very beginning of the speech, those in attendance clearly knew something unusual was happening. This was the same Lamar who had been the secessionist fire-eater, and who, from the same platform in 1859, raised the banner of secession shouting, "I war upon your government!" It was the same Lamar who had drafted the Mississippi Secession Ordinance, fought in the rebel army and was part of President Jefferson Davis's inner circle.

Yet, as he continued speaking, the chamber became suddenly quiet. Faces turned and fixed on the singular figure that stood before them, his long hair combed back over his ears, mouth hidden by his luxurious mustache, eyes cast down and arms hanging motionless at his side. He spoke without flair or elegance, unusually absent of the old fiery oratory that had made his prewar career. Instead his words were draped by intentional overtones

L.Q.C. Lamar, 1890. Lamar's eulogy of Charles Sumner in 1874 was seen by many Southerners as an unforgivable betrayal of Southern principles and honor. Lamar, however, saw it as an essential means of personal and national redemption. *Courtesy of Library of Congress.*

of humility and reconciliation. "Shall we not...lay aside the concealments which serve only to perpetuate misunderstandings and distrust," he asserted, "and frankly confess that on both sides we most earnestly desire to be one... in feeling and in heart?" The speaker, Mr. Blaine, sat with his face turned away, motionless, tears streaming down his cheeks. Members on both sides of the aisle simply melted away into tears. Onlookers in the gallery sat with a hushed stillness rarely heard. When he closed his remarks, as if invoking Sumner himself, he declared, "My countrymen! *Know* one another and you will *love* one another."

The chamber erupted into spontaneous applause and rose to its feet. "My God!" declared Lyman Tremaine of New York. "What a speech! And how it will ring through the country." And ring it did. News of Lamar's eulogy appeared in newspapers across the country and it made him famous in a new way as the voice of postwar reconciliation. From then on, he was not simply a representative from postwar Mississippi but rather the mouthpiece of a conservative ideology that would command a large following in the years to come. Patriotism demanded devotion to the Union, he had come to believe, if one truly desired to serve the South in the role as its statesman. It was a political policy that became his credo and guiding principle for the rest of his life.

The years after the war took on a seemingly predestined path of public service for the former fire-eater, a duty he shouldered easily and performed consummately. In 1873, he was reelected to his old congressional seat that he had held before the war, and he served there until 1877 when he was subsequently elected to the Senate—the seat once occupied by Jefferson Davis. By 1885, his reputation well established, Lamar was appointed secretary of the interior (the cabinet post once also held by Jacob Thompson). In what he considered as his life's greatest achievement, he was appointed an associate justice of the Supreme Court of the United States in 1888 by President Grover Cleveland, a position Lamar held until his death on January 23, 1893. Even after his death, posterity still views him in the role he chose for himself, a legacy of political heroism most notably cited in John F. Kennedy's *Profiles in Courage*. As a tribute to her shining son, Oxford, Mississippi, renamed the town's main avenue in his honor, and today he rests only a few blocks away in St Peter's Cemetery.

As personally and publicly redeeming as Lucius Lamar's post-bellum career was, Jacob Thompson found himself a wanted man at war's end. In the wake of Lincoln's assassination, Edwin M. Stanton implicated him as a conspirator after a Toronto hotel receipt was found on the body of John Wilkes Booth, tying Booth to Thompson. A reward was offered for his capture and federal agents flooded into Canada on Stanton's orders to find and arrest him. Knowing that capture meant certain death on the gallows, he sent for his wife, Kate, in Oxford to meet him in Canada. Traveling in disguise and bribing officials to make it through the northern picket lines, Jacob and Kate traveled to Halifax, Nova Scotia, then to Portland, Maine, where they caught a steamer for England, escaping only minutes ahead of federal agents.

Abroad and out of reach of the authorities, Jacob and Kate toured Europe for several years. They were presented to Queen Victoria and were received by their old friend, the Prince of Wales. In Italy, Kate even had marble busts made of themselves and shipped back to America. In 1867, Kate returned alone to a still desolate Lafayette County, taking up residence once more at her father's plantation home on Woodson's Ridge, where she and Jacob had met and fallen in love years ago. Jacob was still abroad when he learned he

Jacob Thompson, 1859. Formally charged in 1865 as a co-conspirator in Lincoln's assassination, he was eventually exonerated after testimony by former Confederate operatives in the trial of the actual conspirators failed to reveal any involvement. *Courtesy of Library of Congress.*

had been cleared of any involvement in the Lincoln assassination, returning to the United States in 1868. He was still a wealthy man, having invested much of his holdings in English securities before the war. As if to erase the memory of the turbulent past he helped to engineer, Jacob and Kate left Oxford and Lafayette County and settled in Memphis, where he built her a new mansion and a new life away from politics. When he died on March 24, 1885, then interior secretary L.Q.C. Lamar ordered the Department of the Interior closed in his honor and flags to be flown at half-staff. While he was eulogized as "a brilliant statesman" and "a friend of all classes," his historical legacy remains tainted by the darker shadows of his wartime service as a spymaster.

Both Thompson and Lamar's old friend Frederick Augustus Barnard was a figure whose life after leaving Oxford rose to new heights. In 1864,

After the war, Frederick Barnard rarely ever spoke of his time in Mississippi, which he referred to as "the worst years of my life." Yet he remains one of the most revered chancellors in the history of the University of Mississippi. His portrait still hangs prominently in the observatory that he built and once called home. *Courtesy of the author.*

he became the president of Columbia University, a position he held until a year before his death in 1889. Under Barnard, Columbia grew rapidly, establishing new academic departments, more graduate study and research and a sevenfold increase in enrollment. He also became an author of scientific treatises and a pioneer in providing educational opportunities to women, the result of which—Barnard College—was established after his death and named in his honor. It has since become one of America's preeminent colleges for women.

Rebecca and Alexander Pegues could only pick up the pieces of their shattered life at war's end. Their plantation was a shambles, their money gone and their lives in complete ruin. Half of their former slaves had run off and the remaining wouldn't work. "The war is over, and we are beaten," a disconsolate Alexander wrote to Frederick Barnard in June 1865. "The negroes are in open rebellion," Rebecca noted fearfully in her diary. Eventually, they rebuilt and farmed the plantation, paying their former slaves wages to help work it. In her frantic flight to leave the plantation in late November 1862, Rebecca had inadvertently dropped one of the many diary books she kept. Realizing its loss, she had given up all hope of ever seeing it again. But upon her return to Oxford after the war, a package came in the mail containing the lost book. Inside its front cover, a Yankee lieutenant colonel had written, "This journal was found close to a deserted dwelling near the town of Oxford, Mississippi. The high literary attainments and pure Christian character of the writer led me to resolve that should I survive this war, I will return it to its owner." Rebecca's diaries, which span forty-six years, remain one of the most comprehensive records of daily life in the antebellum South.

The former Lafayette County slaves found freedom a mixed blessing. For field hands who knew only hard labor, the benefits of freedom were manifest. But for house servants, freedom often meant leaving the relative comfort of their master's homes or, if they stayed, having to suffer economic deprivation along with them. When freedom came for Lucindy Hall Shaw, she was plowing in the fields when she noticed a lone rider in a Confederate uniform approach. The man was Mister Jimmie, one of her master's relatives, who told Lucindy the war was finally over. "You kin lay in bed now an' sleep til ten o'clock if you want," the man said. An amazed Lucindy threw down her plow. "He wuz jus' plain Jimmie now," she remarked to Mrs. Minnie Holt, who interviewed her in 1936.

"I didn't have to call him Marster no mo'."

BIBLIOGRAPHY

BOOKS

Baldwin, Thomas. *New and Complete Gazetteer of the United States*. Philadelphia: Lippincott, Grambo, 1854.

Blassingame, John, ed., *Slave Testimony*. Baton Rouge: Louisiana State University Press, 1977.

Bowen, Catherine Drinker. *Miracle at Philadelphia: The Story of the Constitutional Convention May to September 1787*. Boston: Little Brown, 1986.

Boyd, Cyrus F. *The Civil War Diary of Cyrus F. Boyd, Fifteenth Iowa Infantry 1861–1863*. Baton Rouge: Louisiana State University Press, 1998.

Brown, Maud Morrow. *The University Greys, Company A, Eleventh Mississippi Regiment, Army of Northern Virginia, 1861–1865*. Richmond, VA: Garrett and Massie, 1940.

Bruchey, Stuart. *Cotton and the Groth of the American Economy: 1790–1860*. New York: Random House, 1967.

Capati, Emelda V. *A County Editor Faces Secession*. Oxford, MS: Academy Press, 1961.

Carnahan, Burrus M. *Lincoln On Trial: Southern Civilians and the Law of War*. Lexington: University Press of Kentucky, 2010.

Cate, Wirt Armistead. *Lucius Q.C. Lamar, Secession and Reunion*. New York: Russell and Russell, 1969.

Chestnut, Mary Boykin. *Mary Chestnut's Civil War*. Edited by C. Vann Woodward. New Haven, CT: Yale University Press, 1993.

Clarke, H.C., ed. *The Confederate States Almanac and Repository of Useful Knowledge for 1862*. Vicksburg, MS: Clarke, 1862. Reprint, Summerville, GA: Brannon Publishing, n.d.

Coffey, Walker. *Confederate Soldiers, Lafayette County Mississippi*. Oxford, MS: Skipwith Historical and Genealogical Society, 1990.

Crisman, E.B. *Biographical Sketches of Living Old Men of the Cumberland Presbyterian Church*. Vol 1. St. Louis: Perrin and Smith, 1877.

Doyle, Don H. *Faulkner's County, The Historical Roots of Yoknapatawpha*. Chapel Hill: University of North Carolina Press, 2001.

Evans, Clement A., ed. *Confederate Military History*. Vol. 12 Atlanta, GA: Confederate Publishing, 1899.

Foote, Shelby. *The Civil War, A Narrative: Fredericksburg to Meridian*. New York: Random House, 1963.

———. *The Civil War, A Narrative: Ft. Sumter to Perryville*. 3 vols. New York: Random House, 1963.

Goodwin, Doris Kearns, *Team of Rivals*. New York: Simon & Shuster, 2005.

Grant, Ulysses S. *Hardee's Rifle and Light Infantry Tactics*. New York: Kane, 1862.

———., *Personal Memoirs of U.S. Grant*, 2 vols. New York: Charles L. Webster, 1885.

Harwell, Juanita R. and Joan Goar Bratton, eds. *Lafayette County, Mississippi Will Abstracts*. Oxford, MS: Skipwith Historical and Geneological Society, 1980.

Hathorn, John Cooper. *Early Settlers of Lafayette County, Mississippi*. Oxford, MS: Skipwith Historical and Genealogical Society, 1980.

Johnson, Mrs. Jeremiah Grant. *The University War Hospital*. Archives and Special Collections, J.D. Williams Library, University of Mississippi, 1912.

Kennedy, John F. *Profiles in Courage*. New York: Harper & Brothers, 1956.

Lamar Rifles. *A History of Company G, Eleventh Mississippi Regiment, CSA*. Oxford, MS: The Survivors Association of Lamar Rifles, 1901. Reprint, Topeka, KS: Bonnie Blue Press, 1992.

Le Grand, Louis. *The Military Handbook and Soldier's Manual of Information*. New York: Beadle, 1861.

Mayes, Edward. *L.Q.C. Lamar, His Life and Speeches*. Nashville: Barbee & Smith, 1896.

Meacham, Jon. *American Lion*. New York: Random House, 2008.

Murphy, James B., *L.Q.C. Lamar: Pragmatic Patriot*. Baton Rouge: Louisiana State University Press, 1973.

Nash, Alice and Christopher Strobel. *Native Americans from Post-Columbian through Nineteenth Century America*. Westport, CT: Greenwood Press, 2006.

Percy, Ann. *Early History of Oxford, Mississippi*. Oxford, MS: Percy Enterprises, 2008.

Rainwater, Percy Lee. *Mississippi: Storm Center of Secession*. Baton Rouge, LA: Otto Claitor, 1938.

Rising, Clara. *The Taylor File*. Bloomington, IN: Ex Libris, 2007.

Rowland, Dunbar and H. Grady Howell Jr. *Military History of Mississippi, 1803–1898*. Spartanburg, SC: Reprint Company, 1978.

Sherman, William T. *Memoirs of General William T. Sherman*. Vol 1. 1875. Reprint, New York: D. Appleton, 1876.

Skipwith Historical and Genealogical Society. *Lafayette County Heritage*. Oxford, MS: Skipwith Historical & Genealogical Society, 1986.Sobotka, C. John. *A History of Lafayette County, Mississippi*. Oxford, MS: Rebel Press, 1976.

Stampp, Kenneth. *The Peculiar Institution: Slavery in the Ante-Bellum South*. New York: Alfred A. Knopf, 1967.

Switzer, Anna Lamar. *The Lamar Heritage*. New Orleans: Polyanthos, 1977.

U.S. War Department. *The War of the Rebellion: A Compilation of the Official Records of the Union and Confederate Armies*. 128 vols. Washington, D.C.: Government Printing Office, 1880–1901.

Waldstreicher, David. *Slavery's Constitution: From Revolution to Ratification*. New York: Hill and Wang, 2009.

Ward, Andrew. *The Slaves' War*. New York: Houghton Mifflin, 2008.

Wert, Jeffrey D. *Gettysburg*. New York: Simon & Schuster, 2001.

Wilson, Jack Case. *Faulkner's Fortunes and Slaves*. Nashville: Annandale Press, 1984.

Wynne, Ben. *On the Road Histories, Mississippi*. Northampton, MA: Interlink Books, 2008.

COLLECTED HOLDINGS

Aldrich Collection. Department of Archives and Special Collections. J.D. Williams Library. University of Mississippi.

Elijah Fleming Collection. Special Archives and Collections. J.D. Williams Library. University of Mississippi.

E.W. Hilgard Collection. Department of Archives and Special Collections. J.D. Williams Library. University of Mississippi.

F.A.P. Barnard Collection. Department of Archives and Special Collections. J.D. Williams Library. University of Mississippi.

Frederick A.P. Barnard Papers. Rare Book and Manuscript Library. Columbia University Library. Columbia University.

Gage Family Collection. Special Archives and Collections. J.D. Williams Library. University of Mississippi.

Hinton–Longstreet Papers. Department of Archives and Special Collections. J.D. Williams Library. University of Mississippi.

Howry Family Collection. Department of Archives and Special Collections. J.D. Williams Library. University of Mississippi.

Jacob Thompson Collection. Department of Archives and Special Collections. J.D. Williams Library. University of Mississippi.

Jefferson Davis Letters. Department of Archives and Special Collections. J.D. Williams Library. University of Mississippi.

John Guy Lofton Collection. Special Archives and Collections. J.D. Williams Library. University of Mississippi.

L.Q.C. Lamar Collection. Department of Archives and Special Collections. J.D. Williams Library. University of Mississippi.

Minnie Holt Collection. Special Archives and Collections. J.D. Williams Library. University of Mississippi.

Rebecca Pegues Diaries and Letters. Archives and Special Collections. J.D. Williams Library. University of Mississippi.

Journals and Newspapers

Dimick, Howard T. "Motives for the Burning of Oxford, Mississippi." *Journal of Mississippi History 8* (1946): 119.

Kemmerer, Donald L. "The Pre-Civil War South's Leading Crop." *Agricultural History* 23 (1949): 236–239.

Mayfield, Jack Lamar. "L.Q.C. Lamar: A Profile in Courage." *Oxford Eagle*, June 13, 2008.

Memphis Daily Appeal (Memphis, TN). "From General Grant's Army." December 26, 1862.

———. August 12, 1857.

———. September 10, 1857.

———. September 13, 1857.

———. September 15, 1857.

———. September 12, 1860.

Mississippi Free Trader, (Natchez, MS). October 2, 1860.

———. November 13, 1860.

Natchez Courier, (Natchez, MS). November 21, 1860.

Natchez Free Trader, (Natchez, MS). December 1, 1860.

New York Times. "Congress: Exciting Debate in the House." December 30, 1859.

———. "Congress: Exciting Debate in the House of Representatives" December 26, 1859.

———. "Foreign Commercial News," September 30, 1858.

———. "General Markets." January 2, 1860.

———. "John Brown's Execution." December 2, 1859.

———. "The National Crisis," December 27, 1859.

Phillips, Ulrich B. "The Economic Cost of Slaveholding in the Cotton Belt." *Political Science Quarterly* 20 (1905).

Oxford Intelligencer. "The Assumed Right of Secession," September 26, 1860.

———. "Catechism for the South." November 28, 1860.

———. "The Election and the Future." November 14, 1860.

———. "He Is a Friend of the South." September 5, 1860.

———. "The Lamar Rifles." December 5, 1860.

———. "Letter from Chancellor Barnard." August 8, 1860.

———. "Letter from Dr. Barnard." July 25, 1860.

———. "Letter from Hon. Jacob Thompson, Secretary of the Interior." June 6, 1860.

———. "Mass Meeting," November 28, 1860.

———. "Military Meeting Last Saturday." January 9, 1861.

———. "The Mississippi Convention." January 30, 1861.

———. "A Mississippi Flag." December 5, 1860.

———. "Mississippi Is Out!" January 9, 1861.

———. "Regular Convention Ticket! Hon. L.Q.C. Lamar, Dr. Thos. D. Isom." December 12, 1860.

———. "Resolutions of the Mississippi Convention of 1831." November 21, 1860.

———. "A Salute in Oxford." April 17, 1861.

———. "Secession Becoming Epidemic." January 16, 1861.

———. "The Secession Spirit in Lafayette." January 6, 1861.

———. "Shall We Trust Again Those who Have Deceived Us?" November 21, 1860.

———. "Speech of the Hon. Jeff. Davis." October 3, 1860.

———. "The Speech of Hon. L.Q.C. Lamar." August 22, 1860.

———. "Submission to Lincoln," December 5, 1860.

———. "To My Constituents." July 11, 1860.

———. "University of Mississippi: Commencement Exercises." June 6, 1860.

———. "University of Mississippi: Commencement Exercises." July 4, 1860.

———. "University of Mississippi: Faculty." September 5, 1860.

———. "What Northern Black Republicans Think of Douglas." August 15, 1860.

———. "What Shall Be Done?" November 14, 1860.

———. "Wait for an Overt Act." November 21, 1860.

Oxford Mercury. "An Event in Oxford" March 14, 1861.

———. "Forces for the Defence of the Southern Confederacy." March 14, 1861.

Richmond Daily Examiner (Richmond, VA). June 3, 1861.

Smith, E.A. "Confederate Column." *Oxford Eagle.* May 19, 1910.

Vicksburg Sun (Vicksburg, MS). November 19, 1860.

Vicksburg Whig (Vicksburg, MS). November 14, 1860.

Weekly Mississippian (Jackson, MS). November 14, 1860.

MANUSCRIPT COLLECTIONS

Brown, Maud Morrow. "What Desolations! At Home in Lafayette County, Mississippi." Manuscript. Mississippi Department of Archives and History, Special Collections Section, 1940.

Hay, Willard Murrell. "Polemics and Philosophy: A Biography of Albert Taylor Bledsoe." Master's thesis, University of Tennessee, 1971.

Huff, Francis R. "The Relationship of Oxford and the University of Mississippi, 1848–1947." Master's thesis, University of Mississippi, 1947.

Lyles, Samuel Theron. "Conditions Relating to Sectionalism in Mississippi from 1838 to 1862." Master's thesis, University of Mississippi, 1932.

Oldham, Dorothy Z. "The Life of Jacob Thompson." Master's thesis, University of Mississippi, 1930.

OFFICIAL PRINTED SOURCES

Allen, Thomas, comp., *Compendium of the Inhabitants and Statistics of the United States as Obtained at the Department of State from Returns of the Sixth Census, by Counties and Principal Towns, Exhibiting the Population, Wealth and*

Resources of the County. Washington, D.C.: Government Printing Office, 1841, page 37.

Biographical Directory of the United States Congress, 1774–2005: Bicentennial Edition. Washington: Government Printing Office, 1989.

Dictionary of American Biography. New York: Charles Scribner's Sons, 1960.

Journal of the Mississippi State Convention (and ordinances and resolutions adopted March, 1861. Jackson: Mississippi Secession Convention, 1861.

President Jackson's Message to Congress, "On Indian Removal." *Records of the United States Senate, 1789–1990*, Record Group 46. Washington D.C.: National Archives and Records Administration, n.d.

Record of the Testimony and Proceedings, in the Matter of the Investigation by the Trustees of the University of Mississippi, on the 1st and 2nd of March, 1860, of the Charges Made by H.R. Branham, against the Chancellor of the University. Jackson: Mississippian, 1860.

U.S. Bureau of the Census. *Fifth Census of the United States, 1830*. Washington D.C.: National Archives and Records Administration, 1830.

U.S. Bureau of the Census. *Sixth Census of the United States, 1840*. Washington D.C.: National Archives and Records Administration, 1840.

U.S. Bureau of the Census. *Seventh Census of the United States, 1850*. Washington D.C.: National Archives and Records Administration, 1850.

U.S. Bureau of the Census. *Eighth Census of the United States, 1860*. Washington D.C.: National Archives and Records Administration, 1860.

INTERVIEWS

Foote, Shelby. By Jon Rawl, *Rebel Forrest*, September 6, 2002.

Uffner, Audrey (PhD candidate, University of Mississippi). Discussion of Jacob Thompson and L.Q.C. Lamar with the author, March 26, 2010.

OTHER SOURCES

Ginn, Micah and Matthew Nothelfer. *The University Greys: From Student to Soldiers*. DVD. Directed by Micah Ginn. Oxford, MS: Grandaddy's Farm Productions, 2005.

INDEX

ABOUT THE AUTHOR

Stephen Enzweiler is a journalist and magazine writer. Originally from Cincinnati, Ohio, he began his career at age fifteen writing articles for the local papers. After earning a degree in journalism, he worked for a few years on newspapers before leaving home to join the Air Force to fly as a navigator. During his time in the service, he became witness to history itself while serving in the Persian Gulf War and the Balkans conflict. During a break from service in the 1990s, he became the editor of several magazines and also taught art and creative writing. In 2003, he was once more sent to war in Iraq and Afghanistan, where his personal experiences became the basis for a collection of writings called *War Diary*.

Today, he is senior editor and book critic for *Y'all* magazine in Oxford, Mississippi, and writes extensively about Mississippi and the South.